STOP THE  F!

Stop the Rollercoaster
I Want to Get Off!

RONALD DUNN

KINGSWAY PUBLICATIONS
EASTBOURNE

First published in the United States
under the title *Any Christian Can!* by Master's Press Inc. 1976.
Then under the title *Victory* by Tyndale House Publishers Inc.
1984

First British edition 1999

Unless otherwise indicated, biblical quotations are from
the New American Standard Bible © The Lockman Foundation
1960, 1962, 1963, 1968, 1971, 1972, 1973.
Also used is *The New Testament in the Language of the People*,
by Charles B. Williams © 1937, 1966 by Edith Williams.
Moody Press, Moody Bible Institute of Chicago.

ISBN 0 85476 811 4

Designed and produced by Bookprint Creative Services
P.O. Box 827, BN21 3YJ, England for
KINGSWAY PUBLICATIONS
Lottbridge Drove, Eastbourne, E Sussex BN23 6NT.
Printed in Great Britain

DEDICATION

to
the members and staff of the
MacArthur Boulevard Baptist Church
of Irving, Texas,
with whom it was my great joy
to serve nine years as Pastor.
—For saying one memorable night in April:
'If you're crossing over, we want to go with you.'
—For saying one triumphantly tragic holiday:
'We're here, we care.'

and to
Joanne Gardner
my friend and associate
for over thirty years.

Contents

Introduction

Anything Would Be Better Than This!

I once heard Stuart Briscoe compare the life of the average Christian to an old iron bedstead – 'firm on both ends but sagging in the middle'! The statement intrigued me, not because it was catchy but because it described perfectly my own Christian life. I knew I had been saved – firm on that end. I knew that when I died I would go to heaven – firm on that end. But, boy, was the middle sagging! I was on my way to heaven, but I wasn't having a heavenly time getting there.

I was the 'successful' pastor of a large and growing church in a booming suburban area. We would have had to lock the doors to keep from growing. But my success was like that of a slimming aid salesman whose customers lose weight while he gets fatter and fatter. My preaching was helping everyone but the preacher.

I was in good company. Many of the preachers I knew were in the same boat. But that provided little comfort and I often cried to the Lord, 'There has to be more to it than this. I don't know what I need, Lord, but I need something. Anything would be better than this.'

As always happens when we become desperate enough, the Lord answered that prayer. This book is the outgrowth of what he taught me in response to my prayer.

I am indebted to the people at Master's Press for their patient assistance; to my sister-in-law, Mrs Julie Blevins, for an invaluable suggestion; and to my wife, Kaye, who always encourages me and who spent many long hours correcting and typing the manuscript.

God desires that every Christian should experience the life of victory. While the Bible admits defeat, it never assumes it. The predominant theme throughout Scripture is *victory*, and anyone living less than victoriously is falling short of the divine intention.

One of the clearest pictures of the life of victory is found in God's dealings with Israel. Paul tells us in Romans 15: 4: 'For whatever was written in earlier times was written for our instruction, that through perseverance and the encouragement of the Scriptures we might have hope.' And again in 1 Corinthians 10:11, describing their wilderness experiences, he says: 'Now these things happened to them as an example, and they were written for our instruction, upon whom the ends of the ages have come.'

The book of Joshua is God's object lesson on victorious living. It tells how Joshua, taking charge after the death of Moses, led the people out of the wilderness of defeat into the Canaan of victory. And the amazing thing is this – we move out of our defeat into victory the same way Israel did. God's *modus operandi* for a full and exciting Christian life is revealed in this book.

Come with me on a journey with Joshua into a land of abundance. We will cross a river spilling over its banks in flood, watch massive city walls fall at our shout of victory, see dread giants overcome – all pointing towards the victorious life awaiting every Christian. It is not only Joshua's journey – it is yours and mine.

1

The Real Thing

A preacher I know was speaking at a Bible conference on the theme of victorious living and was invited to be interviewed on one of the local radio stations. After introducing him to the radio audience, the interviewer said, 'Now, Doctor, you call what you preach the "victorious life"; is that correct?'

'No,' said the preacher, 'that's not what I call it.'

'Oh, I see. Well, then, you call it the "deeper life"; is that correct?'

'No, sir, that's not what I call it.'

The announcer started to speak, hesitated, then asked, 'Doctor, what *do* you call what you preach?'

'I call it the Christian life,' the preacher answered.

My friend was right. A victorious life is not a superior brand of Christianity reserved for the elite of the elect. It is the normal life for every Christian. It isn't bestowed upon some because they are spiritual; it is given to all because they are saved! Too many Christians are struggling to win a victory that has already been won. It was won 2,000 years ago. The Christian life is a victorious life, and anything less is a cheap imitation of the real thing. Jesus said, 'I came that they might have life, and might have it abundantly' (John 10:10).

It will help if we understand that the Christian life can be divided into two stages, the Red Sea stage and the River Jordan stage, with a wilderness in between. What the cross is to us, the Red Sea was to Israel. It was the symbol of their redemption, their deliverance from the bondage of Egypt by the mighty hand of God. They looked back to the Red Sea as we look back to the cross; they celebrated the Passover as we celebrate the Lord's Supper.

But it wasn't enough to get them out of Egypt. Moses reminded the people in Deuteronomy 6:23 that 'He brought us out from there [Egypt] in order to bring us in, to give us the land which He had sworn to our fathers'. The purpose of their redemption wasn't realised until they entered the land of Canaan. And to enter that land they had to cross the River Jordan. Then and only then would the redemptive purpose of God be fulfilled.

This may surprise you, but Canaan never symbolises heaven in the Bible. Church hymns may say that, but the Bible doesn't. There were giants in Canaan – there are no giants in heaven. There were battles to be fought in Canaan – there will be no battles in heaven. God's people sinned in Canaan – in heaven all traces of sin will be erased.

Canaan represents the fullness of salvation, the fullness of blessing, the possessing of our possessions. Canaan was what God redeemed Israel for, just as victory is what God saved us for. He brought us out that he might bring us in. Many Christians are out but not in. They, like those spoken of in 1 Corinthians 10:5, die in the wilderness without ever experiencing the life of fullness in Christ.

The Old Testament describes Canaan as a land flowing with milk and honey, a land of luscious clusters of grapes and pomegranates and figs. The New Testament describes our Canaan as:

- peace which passes all understanding (Philippians 4:7);
- joy unspeakable and full of glory (1 Peter 1:8);
- blessed with every spiritual blessing in Christ (Ephesians 1:3);
- more than conquerors through Him who loved us (Romans 8:37).

Are you in?

The first nine verses of Joshua tell us three important things about the life of victory:

> Every place on which the sole of your foot treads, I have given it to you. . . . Be strong and courageous, for you shall give this people possession of the land which I swore to their fathers to give them. Only be strong and very courageous; be careful to do according to all the law . . . be careful to do according to all that is written in it; for then you will make your way prosperous, and then you will have success. Have I not commanded you? Be strong and courageous! Do not tremble or be dismayed, for the Lord your God is with you wherever you go. (Joshua 1:3–9)

Victory is the goal of the Christian life

Recently I heard someone refer to the victorious life as 'an emphasis'. It is not one emphasis in the Christian life; it *is* the Christian life. That's why in this book the two terms 'Christian life' and 'victorious life' will be used interchangeably.

As we have already seen, escape from servitude in Egypt was not God's goal for his people. He took them *out* of Egypt in order to bring them *in* to their own

land, the land he had promised them. Generations
before, God had made this promise to Abraham as
Abraham stood looking over the strip of land between
the Mediterranean Sea and the River Jordan: 'Lift up
your eyes and look from the place where you are,
northward and southward and eastward and westward;
for all the land which you see, I will give it to you and
to your descendants forever' (Genesis 13:14–15).
Freedom from Egypt was only the first step. Until they
occupied Canaan they would not experience God's
complete rescue operation.

In the same way, God's goal in saving us is not to
get us out of hell and into heaven – that's just a bonus.
The real goal is for us to experience all that he has
promised us in Christ. This is not an incidental
emphasis in Scripture, but its heart. Listen to Paul
speaking to the Roman Christians: 'For whom He
foreknew, He also predestined to become conformed to
the image of His Son ... ' (Romans 8:29). To the
Ephesians Paul revealed the goal of salvation in these
words: '... He chose us in Him before the foundation
of the world, that we should be holy and blameless
before Him ...' (Ephesians 1:4). Not a word about hell
or heaven there.

Paul wrote to the Christians at Colossae: '... the
mystery which has been hidden from the past ages and
generations; but has now been manifested to His saints
... which is Christ in you, the hope of glory' (Colossians
1:26–27).

In all God's dealings with you, he has been leading you
up to his goal: the full release of Christ in you. That is
your only hope for a glorious life.

Paul makes another point about victorious living in his

second letter to the Corinthian church: 'But thanks be to God, who always leads us in His triumph in Christ' (2 Corinthians 2:14). It is possible for a Christian to be victorious all the time. Since the Lord Jesus can give you victory for a minute, he can give you victory for an hour; if for an hour, then for a day. If he can give you victory for a day, he can give you victory day by day for a lifetime. Anything less than always triumphing in Christ is less than God's desire for you.

But wait a minute. Does living in victory mean we no longer sin? Not at all; but it does mean that we learn to depend upon Christ for every aspect of our life. We live in his strength, not our own. We serve his desires, not our own. We live for his glory, not our own. And when we sin, instead of plunging into despair and guilt, we trust his cleansing blood to wash it away and restore us to that sweet fellowship. We become supersensitive to sin, and when the Holy Spirit convicts us we immediately deal with it.

The best way to define the victorious life is to describe it. So let's examine some of its ingredients.

1. We enter into God's promises

The promises of the Bible become experiential instead of merely theological. God's promises to Joshua were definite. He told the Israelites the land was theirs; they needed only to act — act with strength, courage and obedience. And the promises made generations earlier were fulfilled before their eyes. I'm afraid many Christians look at the promises of God as I looked at catalogues as a boy. When I was about ten I spotted something I desperately wanted in the catalogue and I had to have it! It cost twenty-five dollars, but it might as well have been a thousand. Knowing it was beyond my reach, I would get out the catalogue, turn to the page that displayed the picture of this thing that was 'mine', and dream. No wonder the catalogue is called 'the wish book'. I wished and wished, but I knew I couldn't have it. And to many Christians the Bible is just that – a wish book. They read the promises with enthusiasm and shout 'Amen' when they are preached from the pulpit, but never really expect to see them fulfilled in their own lives. But the Bible is not a wish book; it is a faith book. And for those who by faith cross over into victory, all the promises of God become real.

2. We experience God's presence

One of the promises God made to Israel and repeated often in this chapter is 'I will be with you.' They would experience his continuing presence. God would be real to them. When I was in college, I read a sermon by R. W. Dale, the famous preacher from Birmingham, England, in which he said, 'Christ is as real to me as the chair on this platform.' I thought, 'Wouldn't it be great to be able to say that and mean it!' I knew Jesus wasn't that real to me, but I longed for him to be. But, praise the Lord, when he answered my desperate cry for help, one of the first things I experienced was the overwhelming awareness of his presence. Jesus became more real to me than any chair on any platform!

3. We exercise God's power

God promised Joshua, 'No man will be able to stand before you all the days of your life' (Joshua 1:5). He was telling Joshua that no man could prevent Israel from reaching their God-appointed goal. Joshua would have the power to do everything God asked him to do. When the original spies went into the land, they cowered like grasshoppers before the giants of Canaan. But Caleb, standing on God's promises, declared that the giants would be bread for them. 'Pass the peanut butter! We'll make sandwiches with them.' And a generation later, as Israel acted in God's power, they found him spreading a banquet table for them. God's power gives us victory over the giants in and around us. We become not only giant-defeaters but also giant-eaters!

Resurrection power: 'I pray that ... you may know ... what is the surpassing greatness of His power toward us who believe ... in accordance with the working of the strength of His might which He brought about in Christ, when He raised Him from the dead...' (Ephesians 1:18–20). Think of it! The same power that raised Jesus from the dead is made available to every believer. You're facing a problem. Which is easier – solving that problem or raising a dead man from the grave? The answer is obvious. If God can raise one from the grave, he can do anything. You have resurrection power residing in you.

Reigning power: '... Those who receive the abundance of grace and of the gift of righteousness will reign in life through the One, Jesus Christ' (Romans 5:17). God has made kings out of slaves, and princes out of paupers. And notice, the verse says 'in life', not in heaven. He's not talking about the 'Sweet Bye and Bye' but the 'Nasty Here and Now'!

Released power: 'And for this purpose also I labor, striving according to His power, which mightily works within me' (Colossians 1:29). The life of victory means that I no longer labour according to my strength but according to his. My ability is no longer measured by my power but by his. Throw the word 'impossible' out of your vocabulary. You can do anything and everything God wants you to do. There is nothing that can prevent you from being exactly what God wants you to be. No wonder it's called the gospel – good news!

Victory is a gift to the Christian

Victory is not only God's goal for the Christian; it is also his gift to the Christian. 'Every place on which the sole of your foot treads, I have given it to you, just as I spoke to Moses' (v. 3). Notice the tense: 'I have given', not 'I will give'. It was already theirs. God had given the land with all its riches to his people before they even saw what it was like.

Understanding that the victorious life is a gift already given us by God is essential. This means victory is *assured*. There is no reason why every Christian cannot live a life of victory, because it is not attained by struggling and striving. It is part of your birthright as a child of God. You don't have to make peace with failure or come to terms with defeat. The victory of Christ is yours for the taking.

God's people are often slow to believe this – slower even than non-Christians. In chapter 2 of Joshua, Rahab, an insignificant citizen of the soon-to-be conquered city of Jericho, said to the spies:

> I know that the Lord has given you the land. . . . For we have heard how the Lord dried up the water of the Red Sea. . . . And when we heard it, our hearts melted and no courage remained in any man any longer because of you; for the Lord

your God, He is God in heaven above and on earth beneath.
(Joshua 2:9–11)

The enemy knew they had lost before the Israelites knew
they had won! They had more faith in the power of God
than God's people did.

Since victory is a gift from God, it is already
accomplished. Before Joshua led the people into Canaan,
God said to him, 'I have given it to you.' Though the land
was occupied by the enemy, it was God's and he had
given it to his people. Every step Joshua took was on
conquered ground. And that's what the life of victory is:
walking on conquered ground. Christian, every step you
take today will be on ground conquered and controlled by
our Lord Jesus Christ.

Victory must be gained by the Christian

After going to great lengths to say the victorious life is a
gift, you may think I am contradicting myself when I say
it must be gained. But the Scripture holds to both
concepts. God told Joshua he had already given them the
land but that they would have to possess it, and that would
require strength and courage. Although the gift was
absolute, it had to be appropriated. There was something
for them to do.

This same idea is made clear by Jesus in Matthew
11:28–29. First he said, 'Come to Me and I will give you
rest,' and then he said, 'You shall find rest.' Well, which
is it – does he give it or do we find it? Both. By simply
coming to Christ we receive rest, but there is a second rest
(comparable to the life of victory) that we find only by
taking his yoke and learning of him. Rest is given, but rest

must be gained. There is God's side of giving and man's side of gaining.

How do we gain it? What is our part? Three things are mentioned in chapter 1 of Joshua.

1. The victory is gained by faith

Joshua was to take God at his word and start walking. And that's what faith is: acting on the word of God. 'This is the victory that has overcome the world – our faith' (1 John 5:4). We exercise faith when we acknowledge that the victory has already been won for us by Christ and thank him for it. We don't go out *to* victory – we go out *from* victory. The Christian life is lived from a platform of victory already accomplished. Face each new day with this attitude: 'Lord, thank you that every problem I meet today has already been overcome by you. Every temptation I confront today has already been put down by you.' But if you meet the day hoping you can remain strong and true, determined to do your best for Jesus, you will fail miserably. *Victory isn't doing your best for Jesus; it is Jesus doing his best for you!* You have no victories to win; Jesus won them all. Rely upon him.

2. The victory is gained by following

God told Joshua: 'Only be strong and very courageous; be careful to do according to all the law . . . do not turn from it to the right or to the left, so that you may have success wherever you go' (Joshua 1:7). Here is God's formula for success. God was actually telling Joshua that success in the forthcoming venture depended upon him. You say, 'I thought it depended upon the Lord.' It does, but the Lord can give us that success only as we follow his instructions. A few years ago while on holiday I fell down a flight of stairs and injured my ankle. I went to the emergency department of the local hospital and as I waited for someone to help me I noticed a sign on the wall. It said: 'When all else fails, try following the directions.' That was encouraging. I hoped they would try the directions first. That's what God was saying to Joshua – and to us.

The word translated 'law' means 'directions', and that's what God's law is: divine directions on how to put together a successful life. This will be discussed more fully in the next chapter, but for now let's get one thing clear: obedience to God's directions is an evidence of our faith, and without it there can be no victorious life.

This third point may startle you.

3. The victory is gained by fighting

When the people left Egypt, God could have taken them by a direct way straight into Canaan, but he led them by a circuitous route instead. God deliberately made the journey longer. Why? The explanation is recorded in Exodus 13:17:

> Now it came about when Pharaoh had let the people go, that God did not lead them by the way of the land of the Philistines, even though it was near; for God said, 'Lest the people change their minds when they see war, and they return to Egypt.'

They weren't ready to fight, and entering Canaan required courageous fighting men, so God postponed military confrontation until they were ready.

The land of fullness is occupied by the enemy. We will not go in unopposed. Spiritual warfare is the order of the day when we move into our victory. Have you noticed that while in the wilderness, Israel didn't fight a single battle (except among themselves)? Only when they entered Canaan did they encounter warfare. That is significant.

Again, this doesn't contradict the fact that victory isn't won by our struggling and striving. Although we must fight, we fight in the power of the Lord; we are to be strong in the Lord; we are to put on the whole armour of God that we may be able to withstand all the attacks of the enemy (see Ephesians 6:10–17).

But understand this: there will be conflict and confrontation. The ship of Zion is a man-of-war, not a luxury liner. At times it is easy to pray and to praise the Lord; at others it is an intense struggle. We want always to read the Bible with ease and enjoyment, but sometimes only rigid discipline makes it possible. When our flagging faith falters, our enthusiasm wanes, and our bodies tire, we will need the whole armour of God to throw off the attacks of our adversary.

When a person first becomes a Christian, it often seems everything is easy for him. He witnesses, prays, reads the Bible with radiant and tireless enthusiasm. Temptations seem not to exist. God, as he did for the Israelites, is leading him in the easy way. He is not yet ready to fight. When he is suddenly besieged by difficulties, he becomes frustrated and confused and wonders what went wrong. At this moment Satan may take advantage of his predicament and accuse him of total and terminal failure, trying to convince him that God has surely abandoned him. But God has not deserted him; he has merely enrolled the new Christian in basic training in order to get him ready to fight.

The first victory for Joshua was an easy one. No intense struggle took place at Jericho. The people simply marched thirteen times around the city, played their instruments and shouted; and the massive walls disintegrated. The ease with which Jericho was conquered was remarkable. But the other victories weren't like that. They had to fight and fight desperately. Don't assume because of Jericho that you will need only to shout a little and stage a pre-battle victory parade for the walls of spiritual opposition to flatten before you. As you mature in your victory walk, the hand-to-hand and face-to-face combat suggested by Ephesians 6 will more often be the case.

This has been a long chapter, but it has been necessary to cover the basic truths of the life of victory. It is God's goal and gift for every believer, already accomplished by the death and resurrection of the Lord Jesus. But that doesn't mean that every Christian automatically experiences this victory. There is something for us to do. We must appropriate what God has made available.

Let me illustrate it like this. There's a water fountain in the foyer of our church. It contains cool, refreshing water for those who are thirsty. Suppose one Sunday morning after the service I see you in the foyer on your knees before that fountain. With hands clasped in prayer, you're begging the fountain for water, just one little drink. But nothing happens. And nothing will happen, except that someone may carry you off in a straitjacket. You don't get water from a fountain by begging and pleading. You go up to it, bend over, push the lever, open your mouth and swallow. It's that simple. Jesus invited all who were thirsty to come to him and drink. He doesn't force our mouths open and pour it down us. We must do our own drinking. The fountain is waiting; come and drink.

2

Bridging the Experience Gap

Have you ever noticed the disturbing difference between what the Bible says we are and what we really are?

Not long ago I flew to a northern city for a speaking engagement. A man I had never seen was to meet me at the airport. But when I entered the terminal, no one approached me. Many people were waiting to meet arriving passengers, but none headed in my direction. After a while I was paged over the loudspeaker and asked to meet my party at the airline desk. When I got there I immediately recognised the man waiting for me as one of those at Arrivals. I had walked right by him and he had failed to recognise me. He apologised profusely and said, 'I had your picture, but you don't look anything like it.' That has happened so many times, I just answer, 'Well, that picture was made when I was much older.'

It would be difficult to recognise most Christians from the description of them given in the Bible. I wonder if people would be surprised to discover that we're Christians. Might they say, 'I had your picture in my Bible but you don't look anything like it'?

Let's take a quick look at our photograph. In 1 John 5:4 we read, 'And this is the victory that has overcome the world – our faith.' I used to read that and say, 'Aha, that's why I'm not overcoming the world. I don't have enough faith. If God would give me more faith, I could be victorious.' Then one day I read the next verse and it blasted that excuse into limbo. 'And who is the one who overcomes the world, but he who believes that Jesus is the Son of God?' (v. 5). It's not special or super faith that overcomes the world. It's not how much faith you have, but what you have faith in. The statement is unmistakably clear. If you believe that Jesus is the Son of God, you are overcoming the world. I believed, but I wasn't overcoming the world!

Take another look at yourself. 'But in all these things we overwhelmingly conquer through Him who loved us' (Romans 8:37). The words translated 'overwhelmingly conquer' are difficult to translate adequately. The Greek word conveys the idea of super- and supra-conquerors. The Christian doesn't merely conquer – he overwhelmingly conquers. Most Christians believe we'll win in the end. The Lord is going to be victorious finally. But it's going to be close! It's like a football game in the closing moments of which he'll be awarded a penalty kick and beat the devil 17 to 14! No, that's not what Paul says. It's not the Christians 17 and the devil 14; it's the Christians 100 and the devil 0. By the way, that is not a promise; it is a statement of fact.

One more glance ought to be enough. 'Whoever drinks of the water that I shall give him shall never thirst' (John 4:14). Jesus uses a double negative for emphasis: the words are literally 'shall not never thirst'. That's poor English but great theology. Just one drink of the water of eternal life will put a reservoir of contentment and satisfaction within the believer.

I see your name under the picture, but is that really you? That's sufficient to show the terrible discrepancy between portrait and practice.

So the real question is this: How do we cross the gulf between what we ought to be and what we are? How do we bridge the experience gap?

The key is the word *response*. We experience what God says *of* us when we respond to what God says *to* us. As a matter of fact, all Christian living is simply a matter of response. We were saved by responding to God's offer of grace. We sought him because he sought us. We love him because he first loved us (1 John 4:19). 'You shall be holy, for I am holy,' he says (1 Peter 1:16). And John tells us we are to walk in the light because he is in the light (1 John 1:7).

We live the Christian life the same way we received it. 'As you therefore have received Christ Jesus the Lord, so walk in Him' (Colossians 2:6). The Israelites got into Canaan the same way they got out of Egypt – by crossing a river. Interesting, isn't it? God's method was the same in both instances. That reveals a significant spiritual principle: God's methods never really change. We were saved by grace through faith, and we live by the same grace through the same faith. We entered the Christian life by responding in faith to Jesus Christ, and we go on in the Christian life by continuing to respond in faith to Jesus. Our response becomes the ink with which we write the history of our lives.

The Gospels provide a good example of response that led to success. One morning after Simon Peter and the other disciples had fished unsuccessfully all night, Jesus appeared and asked, 'Have you caught anything?' 'No,' they replied. 'We have laboured all night and have taken nothing.' Then Jesus told them, 'Cast your nets down on the other side of the boat.' Simon could have said, 'Now, Master, you stick to preaching and leave the fishing to us. After all, we're professionals.' Or they could have said, 'We've already tried that spot,' or, 'Our fathers fished in this spot for years and taught us every trick. The fish just aren't here.' Instead, Simon responded, 'We have toiled all the night . . . nevertheless at thy word I will let down the net' (Luke 5:5, KJV). And their obedient response produced a bulging net.

In the first chapter of Joshua we find a threefold response to the word of God that guarantees victory. If Joshua would make these three responses, the land that God had already given to them in promise would become theirs in experience.

Accept God's promises

Someone may say, 'Well, I've done that already. I accept every word in the Bible as the true, inspired word of God.' I'm sure you do, but that's not what I mean. I mean you should accept God's promises for yourself, as your very own promises, as though you were the first and only person to whom God ever spoke them.

God's promises are not limited to past saints

In God's commission to Joshua he tells him that the promises he made to Moses were now promises to him: 'Just as I have been with Moses, I will be with you . . . you shall give this people possession of the land which I swore to their fathers to give them' (Joshua 1:5–6).

The promises didn't die with Moses. God renews them with every generation. You must look at them and exclaim, 'These are *my* promises. God promised them to *me* – not just to Joshua or Paul or Peter or the early church.' In Jesus Christ all the promises of God are 'Yes' and 'Amen' (2 Corinthians 1:20).

God's promises are not altered by time

Joshua was standing at the end of forty years of failure. Think of it. An entire generation had died since God had made his promise. But the years had failed to erode the promises of a God who speaks with eternity in his words.

'Forever, O Lord, Thy word is settled in heaven. Thy faithfulness continues throughout all generations' (Psalm 119:89–90).

Don't let a mere 2,000 years separate you from God's promises!

God's promises are not affected by circumstances

Like a clap of thunder, God announced, 'Moses, my servant is dead.' Exit Moses; faithful and familiar leader, a man with a face-to-face relationship with God, a trusted friend who stuck with them through every bad time.

Enter Joshua, the new recruit! If the mighty Moses was unable to bring them into Canaan, who could? Surely Joshua couldn't expect to succeed where Moses had failed? It was not a very encouraging situation. But God made it clear that circumstances hadn't changed his plans. How could they? He had created the circumstances! God planned Moses' death, brought it about, and was in charge of the funeral himself. Rest assured that God will never create a circumstance that conflicts with his plans, regardless of how it appears. Every circumstance, under the control of our sovereign Lord, only serves to further his redemptive purposes.

The quickest route to defeat is to concentrate on your

circumstances. Thank God, victory never depends upon circumstances. Even if everyone about us fails, God is still faithful. Every adverse situation is a fresh call to believe God. Each difficulty is a new opportunity for God to demonstrate his faithfulness.

Abide in God's promises

The heart of God's commission to Joshua dealt with the leader's relationship to the law of God. You can't read the first chapter of Joshua without seeing how important this was. God made it clear that the only way Joshua would succeed in his task was by knowing God's words thoroughly and keeping them faithfully.

> Be careful to do according to all the law . . . do not turn from it to the right or to the left, so that you may have success wherever you go. This book of the law shall not depart from your mouth, but you shall meditate on it day and night, so that you may be careful to do according to all that is written in it; for then you will make your way prosperous, and then you will have success. (Joshua 1:7–8)

The word 'prosperous' carries the idea of making right and wise decisions. The word of God would give Joshua the ability to make the right and wise decision in every situation and thus ensure success in his appointed task. We must learn this truth. Regardless of natural talent or ability, only disciplined devotion to God's word can equip us to do God's will.

The word of God must be placed first

In the daily life of the believer the Bible is to occupy the place of supremacy; it is to be the law of his life. Notice that the law was set above Joshua; although he was the successor of Moses, the God-chosen leader of the people, he was to give undeviating obedience to God's command. There could not be the slightest neglect or compromise: 'Do not turn from it to the right or to the left.'

Our relationship to God's word is stated by Jesus in John 14:21: 'He who has My commandments and keeps them, he it is who loves Me; and he who loves Me shall be loved by My Father, and I will love him, and will disclose Myself to him.' The key word 'keep' means 'to be vigilant, to keep a watchful eye upon' something. It was used of ancient mariners who kept their ships on course by vigilantly watching the stars and navigating by them. We navigate our cars the same way, keeping our eyes on the road markings and speed limit signs and driving accordingly. We especially keep a watchful eye on the rear-view mirror! Jesus is telling us to keep a watchful eye on his commandments and conform to them. They are to regulate our walk, just as the road signs regulate our driving.

The word of God is to be practised fully

First, it is to be the source of our speaking. God said to Joshua, 'This book of the law shall not depart from your mouth' (Joshua 1:8). The law was to direct his speech and predominate his conversation.

Peter said, 'Whoever speaks, let him speak, as it were, the utterances of God' (1 Peter 4:11). Writing to the Ephesians, Paul said: 'Let no unwholesome word proceed from your mouth, but only such a word as is good for edification according to the need of the moment, that it may give grace to those who hear' (Ephesians 4:29). And to the Colossians he wrote: 'Let your speech always be with grace, seasoned, as it were, with salt, so that you may know how you should respond to each person' (Colossians 4:6). John Bunyan was converted as a result of overhearing a conversation among several women. If someone eavesdropped on you, would your conversation point him to Christ?

Second, the word of God is to be the subject of our thinking. 'You shall meditate on it day and night,' God commanded Joshua (Joshua 1:8a). And significantly, it was this meditating on the word of God that would enable him to obey all that was written in it (see verse 8b). This is the same word that appears in Psalm 1:2: 'But his delight is in the law of the Lord, and in His law he meditates day and night.' Verse 3 reveals the result of such delightful meditations: 'And he will be like a tree firmly planted by streams of water, which yields its fruit in its season, and its leaf does not wither; and in whatever he does, he prospers.'

That's exactly what God said to Joshua. Almost gives you the idea God is trying to tell us something, doesn't it? Well, he is. He is trying to tell us that meditating on the word of God is the secret of spiritual prosperity!

The Hebrew word translated 'meditate' has the overtones of 'humming'. A famous popular singer was asked why he was always humming. He answered that humming kept his vocal cords warmed up and ready to perform at a moment's notice. And our constant humming of the word, meditating on it day and night, will keep us warmed up and ready to obey at a moment's notice. The word of God is to be like a tune you can't get out of your head; it is to permeate your life and be absorbed into your system. Then and only then will you be able to act wisely. When you encounter a situation you don't know how to handle, God will be able to give you unbelievable wisdom, because you have been abiding in his word.

Act on God's promises

I met a man recently who said he had been having a regular time of Bible study and prayer, and had even been memorising Scripture. 'But,' he complained, 'it hasn't made any difference.' After talking to him a while, I discovered he lacked one thing: he had not been acting on what he had learned. It's not enough to read your Bible regularly, memorise it and meditate on it; you must obey it. The purpose of the meditation, as we have seen, is obedience: '. . . meditate on it day and night, so that you may be careful to do according to all that is written in it; for then . . . you will have success' (Joshua 1:8).

Reading the Bible will give you knowledge *about* God; obeying the Bible will give you knowledge *of* God. Many Christians know a lot about God but do not know God himself in a personal and intimate fellowship. It is when you begin doing what you have been reading that your life begins changing. God doesn't give us scriptural knowledge for information's sake; he isn't interested in satisfying our curiosity or scratching our intellectual itch. God is interested in our obedience. And that's the purpose of all revelation. 'Thy word have I hid in my mind that I may amaze my friends' is the attitude of many who aren't the least bit interested in hiding it in their hearts that they might not sin against God.

Obedience is co-operation with God

God had already given the land, but Joshua had to walk across it before he received it. And he was given only as much as he walked across. The same is true for us. God gives you only as much as you are willing to walk across in obedience.

Obedience is confidence in God

It is confidence in his promise. 'I have given it to you,' God said. I have made a marvellous discovery. God never asks you to do something without giving you the power to do it. Our obedience is simply saying 'Amen' to God's promise. Joshua could take the land because God had already given it to him. This means that disobedience is an assault on the character of God; it is saying, 'God, you can't be trusted.' On the other hand, obedience is saying, 'God, I trust you, and to prove my trust, I'm going to do everything you tell me.'

But more than this, obedience is confidence in his presence. Listen to verse 9: 'Have I not commanded you? Be strong and courageous! Do not tremble or be dismayed, for the Lord your God is with you wherever you go.' It is his presence that gives you the courage to obey, even when faced with unbelievable problems and insurmountable obstacles. And he will go with you even more closely than he went with Joshua, because he actually lives within you through his Holy Spirit.

Friend, you hold the key to the door of victory. The key is your response to the promises of God. Use it and you will unlock the vault to all of heaven's resources.

3

Getting Ready to Go

As a child I loved it when the family talked about taking a trip. I remember Dad bringing home road maps of the places we wanted to visit, and in the evening we would spread them on the floor and choose the easiest route and the best points to stop. Of course, like most families, we talked more than we travelled. But occasionally the hoped-for opportunity would come and we'd be off! Do you know how I knew we were actually going? When Mum made preparations to leave. Getting ready to go was the sign – and the best part of the trip! It was also the hardest and most important, often taking longer than the trip itself.

It's the same in the spiritual realm. Preparation is an act of faith. If we really believe God is going to do something, we get ready for it. When we pray for rain we ought to carry an umbrella. In my own spiritual pilgrimage I am discovering that God gives me only what I am prepared to receive.

After God had spoken to Joshua, the new leader came away convinced God would go with them and give them the land. He was so certain of this that he ordered the people to get ready for immediate action. God had spoken and preparation was the evidence of their faith in that spoken word.

The Bible says:

> Then Joshua commanded the officers of the people, saying, 'Pass through the midst of the camp and command the people, saying, "Prepare provisions for yourselves, for within three days you are to cross this Jordan, to go in to possess the land which the Lord your God is giving you, to possess it . . . .Consecrate yourselves, for tomorrow the Lord will do wonders among you."' (Joshua 1:10–11; 3:5)

It is the prepared people who possess the land; therefore, we need to examine the preparations required for the trip into Canaan.

A new diet

'Prepare provisions,' God said. That's interesting. Here is an entire nation, possibly three million people, about to cross a flooding river, and what is the first thing they are to prepare? A bridge? That would seem reasonable. Boats, at least. But without a bridge or a boat in sight God told them to prepare – *bread*.

During the wilderness years God provided manna to eat. Now, if you're stranded in a desert with no other food, manna is all right, but it has been highly overrated in sermons and songs. Manna was a coarse, dry, hard bread – not steak and potatoes. It could sustain but not satisfy. Get this: the diet that was adequate to maintain life in the desert would not nourish combat troops conquering and settling a new land.

Most of the Christians I know exist on a desert diet – just enough to keep them alive. But if you want to move into the land of promise, and experience daily victory, you must upgrade your diet and increase your intake.

I'm talking about your personal worship time with the Lord in prayer and the word. Much has been said about this already because I am convinced that this is the single most important factor in consistent Christian living. How much time have you spent alone with God *today* on your knees before an open Bible? If you're serious about a victorious life, then determine right now that whatever the cost or sacrifice, you will establish a daily time with God in prayer and Bible study. The strength and stamina you have in the conflicts of life will be determined by the quality of nourishment you receive from the Lord.

A new delay

This part of their preparation is even more surprising than the first. There would be a three-day delay. But, Lord, why this delay? We've been delayed forty years already and now we're ready to go. But God said, 'Wait.' One of the things I've learned about God is that he never hurries. The toughest thing I have to do is wait, and I hate it. We are accustomed to instant gratification: instant credit, instant comfort and instant coffee. Our cry is, 'Lord, give me patience right now!' But God never wastes time, and every delay plays an important role in his plan.

God used the delay to accomplish three things. First, it was a time of *observation*. The people had to camp on the banks of the Jordan for three days, and what did they do during that time? They watched the swollen river surging over its banks. 'We're going to cross *that*?' they may have whispered to one another. 'But there's no bridge, no boats! It can't be done!' That's the point exactly.

God was letting the impossibility of the task sink into their minds.

Has God ever dealt with you that way? He has with me. Many times he has plopped me down beside the Jordan of my life and forced me to look at it. The longer I looked, the more impossible the situation became. I would cry out for deliverance, wondering how God could love me and yet refuse to remove the problem. I could see no boats, no bridges, no way of getting through the situation. After a while I would know that apart from God there was no solution. When we are convinced that only God can get it all together, then we're ready to move.

The delay was also a time of *confirmation*. Forty years earlier, twelve spies had been sent out from Kadesh-barnea. It was their faithless report, blurted out in front of all the people, that had caused them to turn back and forfeit the land. This time Joshua sent out two spies, who spent these three days scouting the land. Their report, brought privately to Joshua, declared that God was surely with them – all the inhabitants of the country were terrified of them. God used the waiting period to confirm his promise.

During those frustrating delays, if we keep our eyes and ears attuned to God, he will give us one piece of evidence after another that he is capable of handling our situation.

The delay was also a time of *separation*. While Moses was still alive, the tribes of Reuben and Gad and half the tribe of Manasseh had become enchanted with the wilderness close to the River Jordan. It was fertile land and they wanted to settle down there. They preferred the wilderness. Angrily, Moses said, 'Oh, so you want to let your brothers go on and fight alone for the land God has given to all of us. Well, you can stay here if you want, but first you must go over and fight with the rest of us.' And they agreed. In verses 12 to 18 of chapter 1, Joshua honoured the decision made by Moses and those tribes.

That incident is packed with spiritual instruction. God lets us choose the level of our Christian experience. He forces no one to enter into victory. If the wilderness is what you want, the wilderness is what you will get.

The descendants of those tribes are found in every church. They do their share of the fighting but always return to their spiritual wilderness, refusing to live in the victory Christ has won for them. They help with the budget, the building programme, the Sunday school; they support the pastor and faithfully attend the worship services, but when twelve noon strikes, they tuck their Bibles under their arms and plod wearily back to a barren and defeated life.

The tragic conclusion to the story is that these two and a half tribes were the first to be conquered and carried into captivity when the Assyrians attacked in later years. When the real testing comes, the first to falter and fail are those who choose to live on the wrong side of Jordan.

A new dedication

After the period of waiting, Joshua told the people to consecrate themselves. The last time they had heard this command was when Moses went up to the mountain to receive the law from God (cf. Exodus 19:10ff.). He told the people to consecrate themselves so they would be ready to hear God's words upon his return. This was an old dedication; a lot had happened since then, and they had long since been unfaithful.

Now God was about to do something new, and they needed a new dedication.

'Consecrate' means 'to purify, to sanctify, to make something holy by setting it apart for special use'. There is a sense in which God sanctifies us and another sense in which we sanctify ourselves. By virtue of our salvation, we are all sanctified, set apart for God's special use; every Christian is a saint. But the Bible also commands us to purify ourselves (1 John 3:3), to set ourselves apart from the filthiness of the world; and this is a must for the life of victory.

We must be willing to deal with our sins, to confess and forsake them, and allow God to cleanse us from every unrighteousness (1 John 1:9). Just a casual reading of Joshua 7 reveals the devastating effects of hidden sin in the life of one believer. God demands holiness.

We must be holy in our public lives

Our activities are to be pure. Exodus 19 shows that this process of purification required that the people wash their garments: 'The Lord also said to Moses, "Go to the people and consecrate them today and tomorrow, and let them wash their garments"' (Exodus 19:10). The garments, seen by all, were to be spotless. We are to present to the world a clean life; our activities must be above reproach.

We must be holy in our private lives

Our affections are to be pure. This was symbolised in the purification rite by marital abstinence for a period of time. 'And he said to the people, "Be ready for the third day; do not go near a woman"' (Exodus 19:15). This indicated a complete dedication to the Lord in the most intimate affairs. When we get down to business with God, our private lives will be characterised by holiness. Let me suggest you pray through Psalm 139, especially the last two verses: 'Search me, O God, and know my heart; try me and know my anxious thoughts; and see if there be any hurtful way in me, and lead me in the everlasting way' (Psalm 139:23–24).

It might be good to stop at this point and catch up with yourself. Think about what you've read so far. Are you weary of the wilderness? Does your heart cry out for much more of Christ? Above everything else in the world do you want to know Christ in all his fullness? Are you ready to let Jesus, our Joshua, lead you into the Promised Land? If so, then consecrate yourself and get ready, for the Lord is ready to do wonders in your life.

4

Hark, the Ark!

It's sobering to realise that one day can alter your entire life. In just twenty-four hours your world, with its hopes and plans, can be reduced to ashes — or it can be wondrously transformed beyond your wildest expectations. The direction of world history has often been determined by the events of a single day.

It was that way with Israel. In one day they moved out of forty years of failure and reproach into the greatest era of their history. A nation flat on its back sprang to its feet and marched victoriously into a new land.

What was special about that day? What was the key to their triumph? This isn't an idle question simply to satisfy historical curiosity. Remember that the events of that day were recorded as examples to us. God's methods, like himself, do not change, and to discover the key to Israel's victory is to discover the key to our own.

The third chapter of Joshua relates the happenings of that day. A close study shows that the main figure in the drama was the ark of the covenant. It is mentioned ten times.

And they commanded the people, saying, 'When you see the ark of the covenant of the Lord your God with the Levitical

43

priests carrying it, then you shall set out from your place and go after it. . . .' And it shall come about when the soles of the feet of the priests who carry the ark of the Lord, the Lord of all the earth, shall rest in the waters of the Jordan, the waters of the Jordan shall be cut off. . . . And the priests who carried the ark of the covenant of the Lord stood firm on dry ground in the middle of the Jordan while all Israel crossed on dry ground, until all the nation had finished crossing the Jordan. (Joshua 3:3, 13, 17)

Without question, the ark was the key to their victory. But what was different about it on that day? They had possessed the ark, made according to God's instructions, since Moses met God on Mount Sinai. During the long, bitter years of wandering, the ark had been in their midst, but there had been no victory.

But now, on this day, something had changed. Do you know what it was? *The position of the ark.* Before, the ark had been in the midst of the Israelites; now it was at their head. The ark had always gone with the people, but now the people were to go with the ark. God commanded them not to move until they saw the ark. As it came into view they were to follow it; it was to be kept in sight all the time. When the priests, carrying the ark, stepped into the swollen river, the waters halted and rose in a heap. And while the priests, still carrying the ark, stood in the middle, the entire nation walked across on dry ground. It was the ark!

The Old Testament ark was a picture of our Lord Jesus Christ. He is our Ark of the New Covenant. We have possessed him since the day of our salvation, but possession alone doesn't guarantee victory. It isn't the possession of Christ but the *position* of Christ that counts. The difference between the victorious Christian and the defeated

Christian is not in what they possess. God doesn't have favourites, giving one believer a larger portion of his Spirit than he gives another. We are all complete in Christ (Colossians 2:9). The difference lies in the position the possession occupies in each life. Only when Christ is enthroned as Lord and Leader can we experience his fullness. It's one thing to accept the lordship of Christ as an article of faith and quite another to accept it as a practical, governing force in our lives. Is he Lord? Does he control your actions, attitudes and affections? Is he Lord at home, at school, at work? J. Hudson Taylor was correct when he said that Christ is either Lord of all or not Lord at all. He is Lord of everything or not Lord of anything.

Simply stated, the key to the victorious Christian life is the affirming of Jesus Christ as Lord.

As Lord, Christ is the door to our unclaimed possessions

The land of Canaan had belonged to Israel for years, but they had never set foot in it until they had followed the ark across the River Jordan. The ark was the door to their unclaimed possessions and unexperienced blessings.

What I'm going to say now is the most important part of the book. The victorious life is not an experience or a formula or a certain way of behaving – it is a Person. That person is Jesus Christ; he is the victorious life. Triumphant living isn't getting things from Christ; it is realising we already have all things in Christ. Jesus said, 'I am the door . . .' to abundant life (John 10:9–10). The abundant life is the life of Jesus residing, reigning and released in the believer.

My favourite passage is Colossians 2:9–10: 'For in Him all the fulness of Deity dwells in bodily form, and in Him you have been made complete. . . .' What can you add to completeness? When God gave us Christ, he gave us everything, for all the fullness of the Godhead abides in him. After we've been in heaven a million years, we'll possess no more of God than we do right now. Only the circumstances of that possession will be different.

Think of it like this: Jesus doesn't give peace; he *is* our Peace (Ephesians 2:14). He doesn't give knowledge; he *is* our Knowledge (Colossians 2:3). He doesn't give wisdom and righteousness and sanctification and redemption; he is all these things himself (1 Corinthians 1:30). If we're hungry, he is the Bread of Life; if we're thirsty, he is the Fountain of Living Water; if we're lost, he is the Way; if we're blind, he is the Light of the World; if we're lonely, he is the Friend who sticks closer than a brother; if we're dying, he is the Resurrection and the Life. He's the Way and what we find at the end of the Way. He is the Door and what we find on the other side of the Door. He is the Fountain and the Water that flows from the Fountain. He is the cause of his own effect and the effect of his own cause; he is the means and the end. He is God's everything to the believer!

My wife has given birth to three children. I suppose the first thing mothers all over the world do the first time they hold their baby is check to see if they are all there! You know – all the standard equipment: ten fingers, ten toes, two ears, one mouth. At birth God gave our three children everything they would ever need to live physically. Lying helpless in the crib, they didn't know what to do with their feet – they didn't even know they had feet. When the time came for them to walk we didn't have to take them to the hospital and tell the doctor to put on their legs. Legs are standard equipment on babies, God's birthday gift to them, even though at the time they can't use them to walk. But the day came when our children discovered that those two things they had been dragging behind them would support them, and, if placed one in front of the other, would take them where Mother said not to go. A whole new world opened up and life was never the same again – for them or for us! Physical growth is discovering what you received at birth and learning to use it.

Likewise, at my spiritual birth God gave me everything I would ever need to live spiritually – Jesus Christ. And spiritual growth is discovering what God gave me at salvation and learning to appropriate it. Like the baby who learns to walk, when we discover we are complete in Christ and learn to appropriate all he is for all we need, life is never the same again.

As Lord, Jesus directs us over uncharted paths

> When you see the ark . . . then you shall set out from your place and go after it. However, there shall be between you and it a distance of about 2,000 cubits by measure. Do not come near it, that you may know the way by which you shall go, for you have not passed this way before. (Joshua 3:3–4)

It has always been God's pattern to lead his people where they have never been. He called Abraham into a far country – he didn't even tell him what country. Joseph went from a rural society into slavery and finally to the ruling seat of a sophisticated culture. Paul, an elite Jew, became a missionary to the despised Gentiles.

Joshua was confronted with a Herculean task – an untried leader guiding an unsettled people into an unknown country. And as if that wasn't enough, the first thing they had to do was ford an unfordable river. How? God's directions were simple: 'Just keep your eye on the ark.'

'*You have not passed this way before.*' I don't know of a phrase that better depicts the adventure of daily living. No one knows what a day may bring. Each day is unexplored territory. No one has ever lived it before. Every person is an amateur. Sometimes it's like walking barefoot through snake-infested grass at night without a torch. This is one of the things that makes life such a terrifying undertaking for so many people.

But we really don't need to know where we're headed or how we'll get there – we need only to watch for the Ark and go after it. Years ago I heard an old preacher say, 'Don't start down the road till you see Jesus.' That's what God was saying to Joshua.

Keeping our eyes on Jesus means we depend upon him. We count on his ability, not our inability. The overwhelming lesson of the Jordan crossing is that the power of God negates the problems of man.

Keeping our eyes on Jesus also means we focus our attention on him and not on the hindrances. And that's the main reason God leads us through unknown territory – he is really leading us to himself. If he had revealed to Abraham the location of the far country, Abraham would have fixed his eyes on the destination and would have determined for himself when he had travelled far enough. Since God alone knew the destination, Abraham had to keep his eyes on God – which is where God wanted them. Of course, we prefer to know all the details of the trip, every hill and curve and turn, but God prefers we know how to follow him. Perhaps this will unravel the mystery of why God is keeping you in the dark about a certain situation. He may be using it to draw you into a deeper and more intimate fellowship with himself.

This makes it necessary that nothing should block our view of him. God told Israel to keep the ark in front of them at a distance of about four and a half football fields '*that you may know the way by which you shall go*'. In other words, the ark was to be clearly visible at all times; nothing was to come between it and the people. Imagine what would have happened if the people had jammed around the ark. It would have disappeared in the crowd, and every Israelite, without knowing it, would have ended up following the person in front of him. Talk about the blind leading the blind! I can picture a gang of them winding up in some dead-end wasteland, scratching their heads in bewilderment, and hurling accusations at one another: 'I was following you! I thought you were following the ark.'

'Not me. I was following him. I thought he was following it.'

'Not me. I haven't seen the thing for days. I was following him. He acted as if he knew where he was going.'

That very thing is happening today among believers. No wonder so few ever make it to the Promised Land.

As Lord, Jesus delivers us from unconquerable problems

While at a youth conference, I heard someone sing, 'Christ is a bridge over troubled waters.' That's a beautiful sentiment, but untrue. Many seem to think that the victorious life is a vaccine against problems. Neither the life of Jesus nor the lives of the disciples bear this out. Christ doesn't elevate us above problems. He isn't a bridge over troubled waters, but he *is* a path through them.

All of us must pass through troubled waters

Not a single Israelite was exempt from the crossing; each one had to pass through the flood. I have no doubt that many trembled as they hurried by the towering mountain of water poised over them. In the middle of your Jordan it doesn't matter that others have been there and safely reached the opposite side; you feel as though you're the only one who has stood in that place. I know; I've been there.

But that's where the Ark is!

Thank God, right in the middle of your Jordan with that menacing wall of water frowning upon you, you find the Ark. What a relief! Surely the water won't crash down upon the Ark. While it's there, you're safe. I don't think you ever know how real Jesus can be until you meet him in the middle of an unconquerable problem. And that is preparation for greater battles. For when you encounter him in your raging torrent, you know for sure he can manage a land full of giants.

I heard of a Sunday school teacher who asked her class of small girls if one of them could quote the twenty-third Psalm. A girl timidly raised her hand and said she could. She stood in front of the class and said, 'The Lord is my Shepherd. That's all I want.'

I think she quoted it correctly. For when the Shepherd is your Lord, he becomes everything you want. That is the victorious life.

5

Dead Reckoning

Many Christians are like a man who comes home and finds his house flooded because he forgot to turn off the bath tap. Frantically he grabs a mop and begins sweeping out the water — *but the bath tap is still on full.* After a few frenzied swipes, he sees he's making no headway against the water, so he gets a bigger mop. Still no success. Determined to live in a victoriously dry house, he enrolls in a seminar on Effective Mopping Techniques, receives a diploma with a gold seal, and once again wades into the battle. But still the water pours out faster than he can mop it up. He invites a professional mopper to come for a week of intensive mopping. At the end of the week, success is measured by the number of gallons swept out — but more have rushed in to take their place. As the situation worsens, he rededicates himself to better mopping, vows he'll never again leave the tap on, and once more takes up the mop. The bath tap is still running.

Weary and waterlogged, he finally concludes that God never intended him to live in a dry house, so he buys a pair of galoshes and a waterbed and settles down to live the rest of his life in a flooded house.

Now I'm not against mopping, but if the tap is still

running, it is a waste of time. The solution is ridiculously simple, isn't it? Stop the flow at its source: turn off the tap.

Application: the water on the floor is our daily sins. The open tap is the sin nature − self − the source of the sins. And the sin nature can produce sins faster than we can mop them up. The secret of victory over sins is victory over self. We've been mopping sins when we should have been mortifying self.

A great many believers have thrown in the towel or, rather, the mop, and have settled down to live the best they can in a flooded house. But God has made provision for a life of daily victory. It is the birthright of every Christian. Don't settle for anything less.

What is God's way to victory? It is not the way we imagine. Man's way is by mopping − training, dedicating, rededicating. But that is not God's way. God has only one way of dealing with sin and that is the way of death.

Israel is poised at the River Jordan, the last barrier standing between them and the Promised Land. Forty years earlier the older generation had escaped from Egypt by crossing the Red Sea. Now the new generation must enter Canaan by crossing the River Jordan. The parting of the Sea was the *way out* of the slavery of Egypt; the parting of the Jordan is the *way in* to the promised inheritance. The first crossing was an exit from bondage; this second crossing is an entrance to blessing. In the first experience the people were saved *from* something; in the second they are to be saved *to* something. The years of wandering defeat in the desert are at an end. They are about to enter into the fullness of blessings God had in mind for them when he brought them out of Egypt.

What spiritual significance does the crossing of the

Jordan have for us today? It marks the end of the self-life and the beginning of the Christ-life. As the Red Sea was a judgement on sin, so the River Jordan is a judgement on self. In the language of the New Testament, crossing the Jordan is entering into the truth that 'I have been crucified with Christ; and it is no longer I who live, but Christ lives in me; and the life which I now live in the flesh I live by faith in the Son of God, who loved me, and delivered Himself up for me' (Galatians 2:20). According to Hebrews 4, we must cease from our own works – the struggles of the flesh – and enter into his rest.

> I struggled and wrestled to win it,
>> The blessing that setteth me free;
> But when I had ceased from my struggles,
>> His peace Jesus gave unto me.

A significant difference in the crossing of the Red Sea and the crossing of the River Jordan is brought out in Psalm 114:3, 5: 'The sea saw it, and *fled*; the Jordan was *driven back*. . . . What ailed thee, O thou sea, that thou *fleddest*? thou Jordan, that thou wast *driven back*?' (KJV, emphasis added). The Red Sea *fled* before Israel, but the Jordan had to be *driven* (or *turned*) *back*. Evidently there was strong opposition to the crossing of Jordan not present at the Red Sea. It was far easier for God to get his people out of Egypt than to get them into Canaan.

It is always easier to get a sinner out of Egypt than to get a Christian into Canaan. In a sense evangelism is easier than edification, salvation simpler than sanctification. It is one thing to bring a child into the world, but quite another to bring that child up in the world. Rearing children is a longer and more difficult process than bearing children. Paul hints at this when he says to the Galatians, 'My children, with whom I am again in labor until Christ is formed in you' (Galatians 4:19).

I remember vividly the birth of our first child. My wife had a difficult pregnancy, but it was nothing compared to the day-long labour and complicated delivery. I have never felt more helpless, more frustrated, more anxious. Travail is the right word to describe what a mother goes through to give birth. But the travail doesn't stop there. While the travail of motherhood lasts only a day, the travail of parenthood lasts a lifetime.

Not long ago a sixty-year-old father came to me with his heart breaking over the rebellion of his son. His son was thirty-nine, with his own wife and children, and yet he was still a source of travail to his father. I remember thinking, 'Lord, is there never a time when we are free of the responsibilities of parenthood?' You would think that when your children get to be adults, are married, and out on their own, you would have nothing more to worry about. But as long as they are your children (and they always are), there is travail.

And in the same way, getting into Canaan is far more difficult than getting out of Jordan. Not that it has to be that way, but we die hard. We want a Canaan with no Jordan. But every Canaan has its Jordan and there is no following of Jesus into his fullness without taking up our cross and saying 'no' to self. Only as we die to self can we live to Christ.

> Soul of mine, must I surrender
> See myself the crucified,
> Turn from all of earth's ambition
> That thou may'st be satisfied?

Yes, that is exactly what we must do, for death has always been God's method. In the first chapter of human history God dealt with sin by death when he clothed Adam and Eve in the skins of an animal. When Israel murmured against Moses, the Lord sent fiery serpents and dealt with the problem by death. Paul uses the tenth chapter of 1 Corinthians to point out that death was God's exclusive way of treating the sin of his people. He summarises by saying, 'Now these things happened to them as an example, and they were written for our instruction, upon whom the ends of the ages have come' (1 Corinthians 10:11).

Even after Israel entered Canaan, God's method remained the same. When they were shamefully defeated at Ai because of the sin of Achan, he and his entire family were put to death.

Let's go back for a moment to the fiery serpent episode. Remember God's strange prescription for snake bites? He commanded Moses to fashion a serpent of brass, fasten it to a pole, and lift it up in the midst of the people. Those who looked in faith were saved. Notice the Lord gave no instruction to treat the snake bites. He dealt directly with the snake, not the snake bites.

Hang on to that thought and listen to the words of Jesus in John 3:14, 'And as Moses lifted up the serpent in the wilderness, even so must the Son of Man be lifted up.' Jesus described his crucifixion as a serpent being lifted up! That tells us two things: (1) the brazen serpent in the wilderness was a preview of the cross; and (2) Jesus' death was a serpent's death.

The serpent was made of brass, a symbol of judgement. What were the people dying from? The serpents. And the only way they could be saved was by believing that the very thing that was killing them had been judged and condemned by God. The serpents were not excused or forgiven or defanged. They were crushed under the heel of God's judgement.

Now what is causing the snake bites of anger and lust and greed in your life? The serpent of *self*. That's why Jesus spoke of his cross as a serpent being lifted up, because when Jesus died, something else died also. The serpent of self, the sinner himself, was crucified with Christ.

This is the only way God can fellowship with man. Even though all his sins may be taken away, man remains a sinful being, and God can have no fellowship with him. The problem with man is not what he has done, but what he is, his fallen nature. And the nature is irredeemable; it resists every effort to improve it and is immune to all treatment designed to cure it.

It is crucial that we understand this: in salvation God does not change, convert or cure the old nature – it is a terminal case. The sinful nature of man never changes. There is only one way God can deal with it: put it to death. Only then can he fellowship with man.

Of course, the old nature resists any effort to put it to death. In his little classic *The Great Divorce*, C. S. Lewis speaks of this issue in a confrontation between an angel and a die-hard sinner. Describing the sinner, a ghost, Lewis says:

> What sat on his shoulder was a little red lizard, and it was twitching its tail like a whip and whispering things in his ear. ... He turned his head to the reptile with a snarl of impatience, 'Shut up, I tell you!' It wagged its tail and continued to whisper to him. ...

'Off so soon?' said a voice.

'Yes, I'm off,' said the Ghost. 'Thanks for all your hospitality. But it's no good, you see. I told this little chap,' [here he indicated the lizard] 'that he'd have to be quiet if he came – which he insisted on doing. Of course his stuff won't do here: I realise that. But he won't stop. I shall just have to go home.'

'Would you like me to make him quiet?' said the flaming spirit – an angel, as I now understood.

'Of course I would,' said the Ghost.

'Then I will kill him,' said the Angel, taking a step forward.

'Oh – ah – look out! You're burning me. Keep away,' said the Ghost, retreating.

'Don't you *want* him killed?'

'You didn't say anything about *killing* him at first. I hardly meant to bother you with anything so drastic as that.'

'It's the only way,' said the Angel, whose burning hands were now very close to the lizard. 'Shall I kill it?'

'Well, that's a further question. I'm quite open to consider it, but it's a new point, isn't it? I mean for the moment I was only thinking about silencing it because up here – well, it's so . . . embarrassing.'

'May I kill it?'

'Well, there's time to discuss that later.'

'There is no time. May I kill it?'

'Please, I never meant to be such a nuisance. Please – really – don't bother. Look! It's gone to sleep of its own accord. I'm sure it'll be all right now. Thanks ever so much.'

'May I kill it?'

'Honestly, I don't think there's the slightest necessity for that. I'm sure I'll be able to keep it in order now. I think the gradual process would be far better than killing it.'

'The gradual process is of no use at all.'

'Don't you think so? Well, I'll think over what you've said very carefully. I honestly will. In fact, I'd let you kill it now, but as a matter of fact I'm not feeling frightfully well today. It would be silly to do it *now*. I'd need to be in good health for the operation. Some other day, perhaps.'

'There is no other day. All days are present now.'

'Get back! You're burning me. How can I tell you to kill it. You'd kill *me* if you did.'

'It is not so.'

'Why, you're hurting me now.'

'I never said it wouldn't hurt you. I said it wouldn't kill you.'

'Oh, I know. You think I'm a coward. But it isn't that. Really it isn't. I say! Let me run back by tonight's bus and get an opinion from my own doctor. I'll come again the first moment I can.'

'This moment contains all moments.'

'Why are you torturing me? You are jeering at me. How *can* I let you tear me to pieces? If you wanted to help me, why didn't you kill the . . . thing without asking me – before I knew? It would be all over by now if you had.'

'I cannot kill it against your will. It is impossible. Have I your permission?'

The Angel's hands were almost closed on the lizard, but not quite. . . .

'Have I your permission?' said the Angel to the Ghost.

'I know it will kill me.'

'It won't. But supposing it did?'

'You're right. It would be better to be dead than to live with this creature.'[1]

The cross saves the sinner because the cross *slays* the sinner. With the cross God doesn't merely take away the sins of the sinner. He takes away the sinner. To remove the sin would only leave the source undealt with, unchanged, and would reduce the cross to nothing more than a 'mopping up' operation. Much more than that occurred at Calvary. So I repeat, not only did Jesus die on the cross, bearing away all my sin, but I died there also. Calvary gets rid of both the sin and the sinner.

'I have been crucified with Christ' (Galatians 2:20).

'Now those who belong to Christ Jesus have crucified the flesh with its passions and desires' (Galatians 5:24).

'If you have died with Christ . . .' (Colossians 2:20).

'For you have died . . .' (Colossians 3:3).

'Knowing this, that our old self was crucified with Him . . .' (Romans 6:6).

'Now if we have died with Christ . . .' (Romans 6:8).

This principle of life out of death is taught by Jesus in John 12:24: 'Truly, truly, I say to you, unless a grain of wheat falls into the earth and dies, it remains by itself alone; but if it dies, it bears much fruit.'

Death is a requisite of discipleship: 'If anyone wishes to come after Me, let him deny himself, and take up his cross daily, and follow Me' (Luke 9:23).

We usually interpret this verse to mean that if we are willing to serve Jesus, we pick up our cross and follow him. The mind conjures up images of a man teaching a Sunday school class with a cumbersome cross slung over his back; or of a teenager handing out gospel tracts on a street corner while balancing a cross on his shoulders. *But a cross isn't for carrying; a cross is for crucifying.*

Jesus wasn't bearing a cross when he preached the Sermon on the Mount. There was no cross on his shoulders when he raised Lazarus or cleansed the ten lepers. When did Jesus take up his cross? Only when he was ready to die.

And Jesus says to us, 'If you want to follow me, pick up your cross and let's go.'

Obediently, we lay the cross across our shoulders. 'Where are we going, Master? To the seaside to teach? To the sick room to heal? To the cemetery to raise the dead?'

'No,' he answers. 'None of those places. We're going to a hill outside the city – to die on that cross you are carrying.'

'Master, we'd rather carry it to the seaside to teach or to the cemetery to raise a dead man – or just anywhere, Lord. But we'd rather not die on it.'

'A cross is good for one thing only,' the Master answers. 'To be crucified upon. If you follow me, you must follow me to Calvary, for that is where I am going.'

As we will see later, following Jesus is a matter of *daily* taking our place of death with him. This is called reckoning.

One more verse: 'And I, if I be lifted up from the earth, will draw all men to Myself' (John 12:32). Here Jesus isn't referring to preaching or evangelistic invitations. He simply says that he will draw all men into his death. He calls men, not to kneel at the cross, but to get on the cross and die with him.

Now let's put all this together under two headings.

1. Our death with Christ was established at the cross and saves us from the penalty of sin.

First, let's establish the time of death. After a service one evening a man rushed up to me and said, 'You've got to help me. I've been trying to die to self but I just can't. I've asked the Lord to crucify me but nothing happens. How do you die?'

'You don't,' I answered.

'I don't understand.'

'Your problem,' I said, 'is that you are trying to do something that's already been done. You're already dead.

You died 2,000 years ago with Christ on the cross. You can't kill a dead man. You must simply accept the fact of your death.'

Paul established the time of our death in Romans 6:6: 'Knowing this, that our old self was crucified with Him.' The word 'crucified' here is a Greek aorist tense signifying a once-for-all happening, something already accomplished. Our crucifixion is an accomplished fact — we died with him. The little preposition *with* is the key here. If we died with Christ then we had to die at the same time he died. When did he die? Nearly 2,000 years ago. Weymouth translates Romans 6:5 like this: 'We share his tomb.'

God views every person as either in Adam or in Christ. If he sees us in Adam, he sees us dead *in* sin. If he sees us in Christ, he sees us dead *to* sin. At this very moment, if we are believers, God sees us dead, buried and risen with Christ.

Free from the charges of sin

It is this fact that saves us from the penalty of our sin. Since we are dead we can never be brought to trial to answer for our sins. Suppose that while reading this book you suddenly hear police sirens screaming down the street and you rush outside to see what has happened. A grocery shop has been robbed. Pushing your way through the gathering crowd, you find the officer in charge and ask, 'Do you know who did it?'

'Yes,' the police officer answers. 'We have evidence that proves George Washington was the robber.'

'George Washington?'

'That's right.'

'*The* George Washington? The one who chopped down

the cherry tree and threw a silver dollar across the Delaware?'

'That's the one. We can prove he did it.'

'Well, excuse me, sir, but you're wrong. It couldn't have been him.'

The officer gives me a puzzled look. 'Oh, and why is that?'

'Because George Washington died in 1799, two hundred years before this crime was committed.'

Do you realise that in Christ you actually died before you committed any of your sins? When the devil, the accuser, approaches God and charges me with sin, God merely looks up my record and says, 'No, it couldn't have been him. He died 2,000 years ago.'

Free from the control of sin

Our death with Christ also makes possible Paul's statement in Romans 6:14: 'For sin shall not be master over you, for you are not under law, but under grace.' Death terminates relationships. It removes a person from the realm of his former activity. Here is a slave, under the absolute dominion of his master. His master tells him when to go to bed, when to get up, when to eat and what to eat; he tells him when to marry and whom to marry. The power of life and death lie in the hand of the master. He must obey; he has no choice. But one day the slave dies. Now let his master shout commands – the slave will not respond. Death has freed him from the slavery of his former master.

The Christian is free. Not free to sin, but free not to sin. The one point of contact sin had with the Christian, the flesh, has been nailed to a cross; the one door of entry has been barred; the one accessible harbour has been blockaded.

'But,' you say, 'if all this is true, why am I still living as though I had never died? The unhappy fact is, sin still has dominion over me.'

This brings us to the next and most important point. You see, we start in heaven and end up on earth. This truth is first positional, then practical. First we state the truth, then we relate the truth. Every doctrine of Scripture must be squeezed into shoe leather and brought onto the stage of daily living.

This is illustrated in Colossians 3, where in verse 3 Paul tells us we are dead; then in verse 5 he tells us to consider ourselves dead. Does that sound like doubletalk? The explanation is simple if we understand the principle of appropriation. In verse 3 Paul states a theological fact, the viewpoint of heaven – we are dead. Then in verse 5 Paul tells us to live like it. Our death is absolute, but it must be appropriated. Our death with Christ must not only be recognised as a fact, it must be reckoned by faith, which brings us to our second heading.

2. Our death with Christ is experienced by reckoning, and this saves us from the power of sin.

In the first ten verses of Romans 6, Paul has established the fact of our death with Christ. Then in the eleventh verse he makes the practical application, telling us how to make this theological fact a real experience, getting it out of heaven and into earth.

'Likewise, *reckon* ye also yourselves to be dead indeed unto sin, but alive unto God through Jesus Christ our Lord' (KJV, emphasis added).

The key word is 'reckoning', a bookkeeping term for keeping accounts, and means literally 'to consider, to account'. Bookkeeping is based on facts, not fables or feelings. The fact is, you are dead. Now consider it so. Let me emphasise again that our death is a fact. Many believers have difficulty at this point because they think they are supposed to 'believe themselves into death', and that their dying depends upon their believing. Christian, you are dead, whether you believe it or not, whether you reckon it so or not. The Bible isn't asking you to close your eyes to facts and act as if something is so when it isn't so. You are dead. That is a fact.

'But I don't know how to reckon,' someone says. Yes, you do. You just don't know you do. In the first place you had to reckon in order to become a Christian. One day you read in the Bible that Jesus died for your sins, and you believed it. Were you there when Jesus died? Were you an eyewitness to the crucifixion? Of course not; you simply believed it. You considered it so, counted on it, believed the fact and were saved. That's reckoning.

And the same Bible that tells you Jesus died, even though you weren't there to witness it, tells you you died with him. Consider it so, count on it and believe the fact. That's reckoning.

You had to reckon on Christ's death to be saved from your sins; and you must reckon on your death to be saved from self. You've been dead for 2,000 years and it's high time you had your funeral.

The how-to of reckoning

Romans 6:11 reveals a twofold reckoning, a negative and a positive. 'Reckon ye also yourselves to be dead indeed unto sin. . . .' That's negative reckoning. '. . . but alive unto God through Jesus Christ our Lord.' That's positive reckoning.

We'll take negative reckoning first. Luke 9:23 tells us how to do it: 'If anyone wishes to come after Me, let him deny himself, and take up his cross daily, and follow Me.'

First, *we must choose against ourselves*. The Williams translation is helpful here: 'He must say, "No" to self.' Our self is always talking to us, insisting we look out for ourselves, demand our rights, that we live our lives the way we please. Self wants only one thing out of life: its own way. And the first step to appropriating the victory of Calvary is to say 'no' to self. Meet every suggestion from self with, 'Not I, but Christ.'

The Greek present tense of the verb 'reckon' indicates that this is to be a continuing process, a habit of life. A thousand times a day we may have to say 'no' to self. Choosing against ourselves is having a 'Not I, but Christ' attitude about every circumstance of life.

Second, *we must consent to our death*. 'And take up his cross daily.' By an act of our will, we must accept our death, and willingly take our place on the cross. We are dead, but we don't want to be buried. We keep postponing our funeral. Having an unburied body lying around can create a pretty unpleasant situation. And most of the unpleasant situations in homes and churches are caused by dead people who haven't been buried.

It is a *daily* reckoning, a daily taking of death to our self, our plans, our wishes, our will. A friend did it this way. He took a piece of chalk and drew the outline of a coffin on the bedroom floor. 'Then,' he said, 'I took my church, my ministry, my plans and ambitions, my family – everything – and placed them in the coffin. Then I actually lay down in the coffin and told the Lord I accepted my death with him. I reckoned myself dead to me and alive to him.' Of course, it isn't necessary to do it that way, but it helped this brother to put it all together.

But we don't stop with negative reckoning. We must go on to positive reckoning. Not only are we to reckon ourselves dead to sin, but we are to reckon ourselves alive to God.

This means that the body is to be used for one thing only: to glorify God. It becomes the channel through which the will of God flows. Paul goes on to say in Romans 6:13: 'And do not go on presenting the members of your body to sin as instruments of unrighteousness; but present yourselves to God as those alive from the dead, and your members as instruments of righteousness to God.'

In 1 Corinthians 6:19–20 it is put this way: '. . . You are not your own . . . for you have been bought with a price: therefore glorify God in your body.'

In positive reckoning we choose in advance God's will for the rest of life. Our body becomes a display case through which he can manifest himself.

It also means that we count upon the life of Christ within us. In Colossians 3:3–4, Paul says we are dead and that Christ is our life. Here is a paradox: we're dead, yet alive. But the life within us is not our own (that's dead and buried); it is the life of Christ, dwelling in us through the Holy Spirit.

As we've already noted in Galatians 2:20, Paul says he has been crucified with Christ, nevertheless he lives – 'yet not I, but Christ lives in me'. If you knocked at the door of Paul's heart and asked, 'Who lives here?' the answer would come back, 'Jesus Christ.' And the same is true of every Christian. When Satan knocks at your door, rather than allowing the old nature to answer reckon it to be dead, and allow Jesus to go to the door. That ought to scare the old serpent away.

I heard Stephen Olford share a motto that he said helps him face each day with confidence: 'There is no demand made upon my life that is not a demand made upon the life of Christ within me.'

And it's true. Every demand made upon our life today, whether trial or temptation, is really a demand made not upon us, but upon the Christ who dwells in our hearts.

Let me illustrate it like this. There are 14.7 pounds of pressure per square inch being exerted on each one of us right now from the earth's atmosphere. The amount of pressure is determined, of course, by how many square inches we are. At any rate, tons of pressure are pushing against us at this very moment. What keeps us from being crushed to death? There is a corresponding pressure being exerted from within you that neutralises the outside pressure.

In the same way, no matter how much pressure the world, the flesh and the devil throw against us, we have overcome them because the Overcomer himself lives within. And his life within is more than sufficient to neutralise the pressure from without. 'Greater is He who is in you than he who is in the world' (1 John 4:4).

Note

1. C. S. Lewis, *The Great Divorce* (HarperCollins 1946, 1977), pp. 89–92.

6

Plugging into the Power

It was going to be a great Christmas. I could hardly wait until the kids saw all the wonderful toys waiting under the tree — games that lit up and buzzed, tanks that fired plastic missiles, cars that raced on a winding track. But as they eagerly ripped open the packages, I noticed for the first time something printed on the boxes: 'Batteries Not Included.' Batteries! It was exciting all right, sitting around staring at immobile tanks and stalled racing cars and ignoring little voices that kept repeating, 'Daddy, this won't work.'

Spiritually, that has been the frustrating experience of many Christians. Time and again, they have had everything but the power. And you might as well try to swim without water as to try to live the Christian life without God's power. If the biblical account of entering Canaan teaches anything, it is that victory demands the release of God's power on our behalf. Knowing how to plug into this power is absolutely essential.

God's power is always flowing. If at times it seems that God is idle, it is only because we have stepped out of the stream. In this chapter and the next we will discuss the streams in which the power of God flows.

God's power flows in the stream of his purpose

God uses his power to accomplish his purposes. It is never released simply to indulge our carnal cravings or to bail us out of a spot he didn't lead us into. God is no show-off; he isn't running a sideshow for the amusement of the miracle-mongers. I was about ten years old when I saw the original *King of Kings* film classic by Cecil B. De Mille. The scene where Jesus stands before Herod brought me to the edge of my seat. Herod kept asking Jesus to perform a miracle, and Jesus wouldn't even answer the old reprobate. As I sat there in the darkness I wanted to jump up and shout, 'Do it, Jesus! Work a miracle. Show 'em who you are!' But he didn't. That was not within his purpose.

We have a tendency to treat God like a glorified butler, or a genie who, when we rub our prayer lamp, materialises to grant our every wish. But he is not our servant; he is the Lord of life who makes plans and executes them. It isn't his concern to accomplish our goals, no matter how right they seem to us. The exercise of his power is reserved for the accomplishment of his purpose. But if we let him, he will sweep us up in the mainstream of his purpose. Then we will know his power. God has a purpose, a plan for every life, and we must find and fit into that purpose. Let's look at three characteristics of his plan for our lives.

It is *an eternal purpose*. Just as God had long centuries before planned for Israel to occupy Canaan, so God in eternity past drew up a design for your life. We are God's 'workmanship' created to do the good works he planned for each of us before the foundation of the world (Ephesians 2:10). Isn't that a staggering thought! Before

I was born, before even the worlds were formed, God singled me out and created a custom-made plan for my life. True success in life is knowing what God created you to do and doing it.

Paul was captivated by the knowledge that God had chosen him before he was born. On the Damascus road he met the living Christ; and as God's purpose began to unfold, he fitted himself into it. Jeremiah was also conscious of God's eternal plan. He first argued with the Lord about his credentials and abilities until God revealed that before he was born, God had known him and chosen him for a specific task.

This perfect plan may include difficulties with which he intends us to live. With the three Hebrew children thrown into the fiery furnace, we must be able to say, 'Our God is able to deliver us. But if he chooses not to, that will be all right' (see Daniel 3:17–18). The purpose of God rises above every other consideration.

God's purpose for our life is *an essential purpose*. It is essential to the fulfilment of our destiny. To miss God's purpose is to waste our life in aimless wandering. God tuned all things to magnify his name. You were created to be a showcase for his glory.

It is essential to our well-being. Our wholeness and happiness depend on our moving towards the goal for which we were created. Diverting our energies towards any other goal drains us of all effectiveness and turns us into misfits in a universe tuned to the glory of God. It's like playing a sensitive stereo recording of a complex symphony on a child's portable cassette player. The music would be a miserable facsimile of what it was intended to be. And if the cassette could feel, it would be frustrated and disappointed with the results.

As Paul stormed towards Damascus to imprison those
who worshipped Christ, the Lord Jesus appeared to him
in a blinding light and said, 'Paul, it is painful to kick
against the goads.' A goad was a sharp, pointed stick used
to keep oxen moving in the right direction. It was painful
for the ox, trying to go his own way, to kick at the goad
instead of yielding to its prodding. Jesus said, 'Paul, why
are you fighting against me? You're only hurting
yourself.' I'm sure all of us have scars caused by the
goads. Oxen have sense enough to stop kicking –
sometimes people do not.

Finally, the purpose of God is *an exciting purpose*. I
doubt that a single Israelite died of boredom. I know that
none of the apostles did. As they plunged forward in
God's purpose, he continued to do wonders among them.
Every Christian who walks with God will find wonders
unfolding each day. Pretty soon, you'll find yourself
starting every day saying, 'Well, Lord, what's it to be
today?' Maybe it will be the contentment of a quiet stroll,
perhaps the turbulence of a stormy battle, or the
satisfaction of giving yourself in service to one in need.

Moving in the stream of God's purpose is exciting. It's
thrilling to see the obstacles collapse like eggshells as
God guides you with his presence and guards you with
his power. When Paul was sailing to Rome, the ship was
engulfed in a great storm. Frantically, the sailors began to
jettison the cargo, but the storm intensified and it seemed
certain that the ship and all its passengers would be lost.
That night Paul held a private prayer meeting, and the
next morning he stood in the midst of his terrified
shipmates and said, 'Cheer up!' (Christians sometimes
say pretty strange things.)

He told them that as he was praying, an angel from

God assured him he would live to preach the gospel at Rome; therefore, the storm would pass without the loss of any life, only the loss of the ship (Acts 27:14—44). God's *eternal* plan called for Paul to proclaim the gospel message in Rome. It was *essential* to God, to Rome and to Paul. And it was *exciting*, to say the least. You and I will find it so in our lives if we're willing to be carried by the current of God's purpose.

God's power flows in the stream of his timing

It's clear from the third chapter of Joshua that a timetable arranged by the Lord was being followed. As this heavenly schedule was kept, the people fitted into the countdown of the Lord. Understanding the principle of God's timing is indispensable if God's power is to be released. Because they fail to recognise this, many Christians have their permanent residence in 'Panic Palace' at the corner of 'Fretful Avenue' and 'Worry-Yourself-Sick Street'.

During a difficult and trying time in our lives a friend gave us a wall clock with this inscription in large letters: 'GOD'S TIMING IS ALWAYS PERFECT.' That clock hangs on our kitchen wall and greets us every morning with its reassuring message. God's timing *is* always perfect. He's never late. Of course he's never early either; he is always right on time.

You can do the right thing at the wrong time. Moses, for instance, knew God would deliver his people from the bondage of Egypt. Having escaped Pharaoh's massacre of Hebrew infants, and having been sheltered in the heart of the king's household, he reckoned he had been chosen to effect this deliverance. And he reckoned correctly. But he got ahead of God and started the campaign by killing an Egyptian bully. I guess he thought he could do the job by killing off all the Egyptians one at a time. He failed to calculate how long it would take or how hot things would get when the Egyptian police discovered the murder. The result was that Moses lost the confidence of his own people (no one trusts a man who works in the energy of the flesh) and spent the next forty years hiding in the desert. When God was ready, the people were taken out in one night.

Abraham missed God's timing too. God promised him and Sarah a son who would be the beginning of a mighty nation. The years passed, but the promise remained unfulfilled. Fearing that old age would cancel the promise of God, Abraham had a son by his wife's servant girl (a perfectly legal way to do things in those days). But man can never bring to pass the purposes of God, and it is a foolish and dangerous thing to try. Nothing but disaster resulted from Abraham's effort to 'help God out'.

Time spent waiting on God is never wasted. We waste time when we refuse to wait upon the Lord and take matters into our own hands. Sometimes the work of God is set back for years as a consequence of our bungling attempts. One of God's most difficult tasks is teaching us to wait. One day a friend of Phillips Brooks, a great preacher of another generation, called on him and found him impatiently pacing the floor. He asked what the trouble was. With flashing eyes Dr Brooks exclaimed, 'The trouble is that I am in a hurry and God is not!'

Jesus' life exhibits the perfect timing of God. The Bible tells us that in the 'fulness of time, God sent forth His Son'. God kept Jesus practically hidden for thirty years before launching him on his public ministry. If we had been in charge of SOW (Save Our World) when Jesus turned up in the temple at the age of twelve, we would have immediately put him on the evangelistic circuit. 'The world is going to hell,' we would have argued. 'You're wasting your time in that carpenter's shop.' But God took thirty years to prepare Jesus for a three-year ministry. God's timing was illustrated by the statement 'My hour has not yet come', which is repeated throughout the Gospels. Several times the Jews tried to kill him, but could not because 'His hour was not yet come'. He always slipped away easily until God said, 'Now.'

On two notable occasions Jesus' timing must have seemed like criminal delay to the others involved. On his way to the bedside of a desperately ill child, he suddenly stopped to talk to a woman about her illness and her many trips to the doctor. Just as he was about to resume his journey, a servant rushed up to the girl's father and told him the child was dead.

Another time, Lazarus was ill, and Mary and Martha, his sisters, sent for Jesus. He purposely delayed a few more days before going to them. When he finally reached them, Lazarus was dead, and the sisters rebuked him saying, 'If you had been here, our brother would not have died.' In both situations Jesus' delays meant death. If Jesus had followed man's timing, it would have saved much grief and anxiety; but following God's timing bestowed other benefits and even greater joy. God always has his reasons. These two incidents, as well as the crossing of Jordan, show us three reasons for divine delays.

God's delays *display our helplessness*. The delay in crossing the Jordan convinced the people that only God could take them to the other side. As long as Jairus' daughter was sick, there was still hope. When she died, all hope vanished. At the time Jesus received word of Lazarus' condition there was still a chance. When Jesus arrived, the brother had been in the tomb four days.

God often waits until things are absolutely hopeless in our lives too. We must be completely convinced that God's power alone can deliver us.

God's delays *deepen our faith*. In both instances of Jesus' delay the level of trust in him was lifted. They already trusted him to heal, but he showed them they could trust him for even more: the restoration of life. When there was no longer any human reason to believe, Jesus urged them to believe anyway. Real faith operates when we have nothing to cling to but the bare promise of God. God uses delays to create situations in which, like muscles, our faith is exercised. Just as exercise strengthens our physical muscles, so the exercise of faith strengthens our spiritual muscles. Without an exercise programme imposed upon us through delay, we would never grow stronger.

God's delays *demonstrate his glory*. Which glorifies God more: healing a sick man or raising a dead man? Leading you across a calm and shallow Jordan or making a dry path through a raging one? This is why God lets things get blacker: it causes his glory to stand out more clearly. It must be obvious that he has done it. Then he will be seen as unsurpassingly glorious, and his people will praise him in the temple and trust him in trouble.

If God is to release his power in your life, you must fling yourself wholeheartedly into the stream of his purpose and wait with steadfast expectancy for him to do his work.

7

Every Christian Must

A car may have a tankful of petrol, but unless the fuel is ignited it won't move an inch. I know many Christians whose tanks are full but they are still stalled between the Red Sea and the River Jordan. For years I was puzzled by members of my church who knew the Bible like scholars, could hear a sin drop a mile away, travelled hundreds of miles to attend Bible conferences, but whose lives lacked the plus of Christlikeness. In spite of all their knowledge and activity there was no sign of spiritual maturity. Love, joy, peace and the other characteristics of a spiritual life were conspicuously absent. They had plenty of fuel — high octane stuff at that — but no spark to ignite it.

The purpose and timing of God constitute the fuel of victory in the Christian life. And the spark that ignites it, releasing it as a practical and powerful force in the life, is obedience. God's power flows in the stream of our obedience.

These first two conditions for experiencing God's power, his purpose and timing, are God's business alone. They are his responsibility entirely. God never consults with us about either his purpose or his schedule. But obedience is our responsibility. Even though the ability to obey comes from God, we, and we alone, are accountable for obedience. When the time is right, God reveals to us his purpose, then says, 'Now it's your move.' And at that moment, everything hinges upon our obedience. We dealt with obedience in Chapter 2. In this chapter I want to look more deeply into the nature of it.

What motivates us to obey God – what is its basis? The record of the Jordan crossing is a testimony to the unquestioning and unhesitating obedience of Joshua. Under such adverse and pessimistic circumstances, how was he able to obey so admirably? The answer is actually simple: he trusted God. Obedience is the evidence and expression of our faith in God. Obedience is faith turned inside out. Faith is the seed, and obedience is the flower that springs from it. Faith is the root; obedience is the fruit. There is a very interesting passage in Scripture in Hebrews 3. The inspired author is recounting Israel's failure to enter into Canaan: 'And to whom did He swear that they should not enter His rest, but to those who were disobedient? And so we see that they were not able to enter because of unbelief' (Hebrews 3:18–19).

In verse 18 he says they couldn't enter because of disobedience. In verse 19 he says unbelief was the cause. Well, which was it: disobedience or unbelief? It was both, for obedience and faith are two sides of the same coin. You act on what you believe and you obey whom you trust. If you were to ask the Sunday morning worshippers if they believe the Bible from cover to cover, probably all would say they do. Yet, the truth is, you believe only as much of the Bible as you are obeying! What you don't obey, you don't believe.

Not long ago, a friend phoned and asked me, 'Will you do me a favour?'

'What is it?' I asked.

'Hey, come on,' he said. 'Will you do me a favour?'

'Tell me what it is first.'

'What's the matter? Don't you trust me?'

I laughed and said, 'Nope.'

Get the point? I was joking with him, of course, but if I really trusted him, I wouldn't be afraid to commit myself to him. If we are reluctant to give unquestioning obedience to God, it is because we don't really trust him.

That leads to another question: If obedience comes from trust, where does trust come from? And the answer is: knowledge. You won't obey someone you don't trust, and you can't trust someone you don't know. So here is the spiritual equation for obedience: *knowledge of God equals faith in God equals obedience to God.*

When Joshua unfolded God's plan to the people, a plan that called for bold and resolute obedience, he made several references to the character of God who was commanding them. He was saying, 'Don't be afraid to do what God tells you; you can trust him.'

He is the Lord of all the earth

This title appears in verse 11 of chapter 3: 'Behold, the ark of the covenant of the Lord of all the earth . . .' and again in verse 13: 'And it shall come about when the soles of the feet of priests who carry the ark of the Lord, the Lord of all the earth. . . .' This phrase indicates the sovereign authority of God. He is the supreme ruler of the whole earth. Therefore, it is his right to command. He has the right to command not only me but also nature, for he is the Lord of all the earth. He is Lord of the Jordan as well as Lord of the Jews. Praise God, if he commands you to walk across Jordan, he will command the Jordan to get out of your way!

He is the living God

'And Joshua said, "By this you shall know that the living God is among you, and that He will assuredly dispossess from before you the Canaanite ..."' (Joshua 3:10). Because he is a living God, he is aware of our circumstances. He is not an unfeeling, uncaring God of wood or stone, but a living God who in all our affliction is afflicted too.

Not only is he aware of our circumstances; he is active in them. The evidence that he is living, Joshua said, is that he will make enemies flee from us. 'Resist the devil and he will flee from you,' James 4:7 declares. A beautiful picture of God's activity on our behalf appears in chapter 5 of Joshua. Just before the battle of Jericho, Joshua meets a man standing in his path with a sword in his hand. Joshua goes up to him and asks, 'Are you on our side or theirs?' And the man answers, 'Neither. I have come as captain of the host of the Lord.' The man, who I believe was the Lord Jesus in a preincarnation appearance, was actually saying, 'I haven't come to take sides – I have come to take over!'

'When the enemy shall come in like a flood, the Spirit of the Lord shall lift up a standard against him' (Isaiah 59:19b, KJV).

He is a covenant God

The ark is described as the 'ark of the covenant' seven times in chapter 3. Obviously this phrase held a special significance to the Israelites. A covenant is an agreement, a binding contract. The Lord of the earth entered into a contract with Israel in which he committed himself to them as their God to act on their behalf. The covenant was originally made with Abraham and sealed by blood. Since the covenant was a contract between two parties with mutual responsibilities, the law was given to spell out Israel's covenant responsibilities.

The two tablets of stone containing the law were carried in the ark; so when Israel followed the ark, they followed the visible reminder that God loved them and had committed himself to them. When Jesus ate the Last Supper with his disciples, he lifted the cup and declared that his blood was the blood of the new covenant. By his death on the cross, Jesus has bound himself to us and has made himself available to our needs.

Any Christian can live in victory, but in order to do so, every Christian must obey. An old hymn says it like this:

> Trust and obey, for there's no other way,
> To be happy in Jesus
> But to trust and obey.

8

It's the Follow-Through That Counts

I love to play tennis but I have a big problem with my follow-through. When I hit the ball, instead of bringing the racket on through to complete the swing, I stop – and the ball sails out of bounds. I just can't remember to follow through. That's why I gave up golf. In every sport, following through seems to be necessary. A few days ago I was watching a Little League baseball game. The pitcher, who looked about seven or eight years old, was having a tough time getting the ball across. After a bad pitch, his mother yelled from the sidelines, 'Follow through, Greg! Follow through!' I keep hoping I'll find a sport that doesn't require follow-through.

I spent a lot of time looking for a spiritual experience like that too – you know, one that didn't require any follow-through. I prefer to be swept along effortlessly in my Christian walk. But that's not the way it works. And some great spiritual experiences faded into nothingness because I failed to follow through. For many, the Christian life is like a soap box derby. Someone gives you a big shove down a steep hill and you're sailing. The wind whistles in your ears, the people sweep by, and everything's great. Then suddenly you begin to slow down. You get slower and slower until finally you stop. You're stalled until you find another hill and someone to give you another push.

A lot of people are stalled in the wilderness, hoping God will come along and give them a big push that will propel them into a big, beautiful experience. The roadside is littered with countless Christians who used to be 'really switched on' for the Lord. Most of them are there because they didn't follow through.

The Bible has a lot to say about this. Paul, for instance, emphasised the walk of the Christian: 'As you therefore have received Christ Jesus the Lord, so walk in Him' (Colossians 2:6). Most of us in our public testimonies stress our 'crisis experience', but Paul talks about the walk. As the old preachers used to say, 'It's not how loud you shout or how high you jump, but how you walk when you hit the ground.' Amen, brother.

The importance of follow-through is also seen in the fact that only four chapters in Joshua deal with the actual entering of the land. The other twenty relate what happened after the entrance. And a very strange thing happened first. Because they were crossing at one of the most strongly fortified areas of Canaan, about 40,000 of the Israelites entered the land dressed for battle – but fighting was not their first act. Though they were vulnerable at that location and ready to fight, God ordered them to stop in that exposed area and worship him by erecting a memorial. Each tribe was directed to take a stone from the middle of the river, one for each of the twelve tribes, and set them up in their encampment. This place became known as Gilgal – the place of passage. The stones, probably placed carefully in a circle, stood as a memorial to what God had done for his people that day.

The Israelites had had a great crisis experience, and the strange circle of stones was their follow-through – and the guarantee that the experience would last. Investigating the meaning of these stones will provide some profitable help for our own follow-through. 'What mean these stones?' (Joshua 4:21b, KJV).

The stones were the evidence of a lasting experience

The monument of stones was there 'so that you may fear the Lord your God forever' (Joshua 4:24). The miracle of Jordan was to have a permanent effect on Israel. There was no doubt that the mighty display of divine power produced instant reverence for the Lord; but that experience was to be so deep, so intense, that such reverence would last for ever. And, I must add, that reverence was to be independent of his miracles. In other words, if God had to keep performing miracles to sustain their reverence, the experience was defective.

It is impossible to have a genuine encounter with God and remain the same. Look at Moses. Meeting God at the burning bush revolutionised and reversed his whole life. Jacob's experience at Bethel wrought such a change in him, God gave him a new name. The Damascus road confrontation turned Saul of Tarsus into Paul the apostle – a change so extraordinary that the Christians could not believe it at first. Those twelve stones proclaimed the beginning of a new era for Israel. But it was only a beginning. That first step had to lengthen into a walk.

This aspect of Christian experience is a major thrust of the New Testament. Paul warned the Corinthians that any religious experience which didn't result in holy living was receiving the grace of God in vain (2 Corinthians

6:1–4). The Galatians made a good start but were in danger of returning to their former religious rut. Staying free was as much a part of their salvation as being set free (Galatians 3:1–3; 5:1).

One of the most sobering statements of the Bible occurs in Philippians 2:16. Having admonished the Philippians to go on to maturity, Paul says, '. . . so that in the day of Christ I may have cause to glory because I did not run in vain nor toil in vain.' What an astonishing thing to say. The fact that they had been converted wasn't sufficient to cause Paul to glory when he stood before Christ. As far as he was concerned (and remember, he was writing under the inspiration of the Spirit) if they failed to follow through to maturity, his labour would be in vain. All his efforts would be meaningless. How could this be? Even if they didn't grow and develop, at least they would go to heaven. Surely that meant something. Not much, Paul said. He felt that if his ministry to them achieved only their entrance into heaven, he might as well have stayed at home. Of what use is a talent in the ground, a fig tree without fruit, a light under a basket? We desperately need to rid ourselves of the false idea that Christ shed his blood simply to buy our way into heaven.

The gospel is frequently described as dynamite, because we get the word 'gospel' from the Greek word *dunamis*, translated 'power' in Romans 1:16. Unfortunately, some of our experiences are exactly like a stick of dynamite: a loud noise, a lot of dust stirred up, over in a second, and not a trace left! We get another word from *dunamis* which I think better describes salvation. It is 'dynamo', a continual source of energy. When God saved us he placed within us a dynamo, the Holy Spirit, who provides an unceasing flow of divine energy, a permanent power supply that enables us to become all God saved us to be.

The stones were to become the centre of their lives

From the very spot in the river where the priests had stood with the ark, from the heart of their experience, they took twelve stones and placed them in their camp. What God had done for them was to be an integral part of their daily lives. Gilgal, the site of the memorial, became the base of all their activities. From there they went out to fight, and whether victorious or defeated, they always returned to that sacred spot. It was the centre of their life.

In the following-through we need a Gilgal, a place of remembering. The stones, like our experience, reminded the people of the faithfulness of their covenant God. It's frightening to realise how easily we forget spiritual matters. We can remember a sordid joke we heard years ago but can't recall last Sunday's sermon text.

That's why the Bible frequently warns us about the dangers of forgetfulness. Thumb through the pages of Deuteronomy, for instance, and see how many such warnings are there. Here are some from the eighth chapter:

> And you shall remember all the way which the Lord your God has led you. . . . Beware lest you forget the Lord your God by not keeping His commandments . . . lest, when you have eaten and are satisfied . . . you forget the Lord your God. . . . But you shall remember the Lord your God. . . . And it shall come about if you ever forget the Lord your God. . . . you shall surely perish. (Deuteronomy 8:2, 11–12, 14, 18–19)

There wasn't any danger they would forget crossing the Jordan and entering Canaan; the danger was that they would forget it had been accomplished by God's power alone. When that happened, they would take God for granted. Witness the defeat at Ai! We all have a tendency to forget our helplessness and God's omnipotence. That leads to living in the energy of our flesh, which, in turn, leads to disaster.

Jesus established the Lord's Supper as a remembrance of his death for us. That's why we call it the memorial supper – like the stones, it is a place of remembering. When we eat the bread and drink the cup we do it remembering that it was for our sins that his body was broken and his blood shed. Remembering the cross is a powerful deterrent to backsliding. Peter tells us that our lack of certain spiritual virtues is evidence that we have forgotten our 'purification from . . . former sins' (2 Peter 1:9).

We also need a place of readjustment. Every Christian, sooner or later, experiences spiritual vertigo and becomes disorientated. Like Joshua, we need a place where we can realign ourselves with the purpose and will of God. D. L. Moody, famous evangelist of the last century, retreated every summer to a private place where he could be alone with God and 'retune the instrument'. Even in the midst of religious activity our hearts can grow cold, and though we may excuse ourselves because we're 'working for the Lord', the heat of activity will not take the place of the warmth of communion.

How can we know we need readjusting? The standard by which we measure our present relationship with God is his previous work in us. We examine our present spiritual status in the light of that past experience. Why not check yourself right now? You remember how it was – the fresh awareness of his presence, the ever-present joy, the love that seemed to flow from your fingertips, the irresistible desire to talk about him. Is it still that way? Is it more so? Or is it less? You used to be patient; now you're touchy and irritable. Moodiness has replaced joyfulness. Worry and anxiety have replaced peace and contentment. Do you find yourself trying to live up to what you were? If so, you need to return to Gilgal, the place of readjustment, the place of confession and forgiveness. William Cowper may have been speaking for you when he wrote:

> Where is the blessedness I knew
> When first I saw the Lord?
> Where is the soul-refreshing view
> Of Jesus and His Word?
>
> What peaceful hours I then enjoyed!
> How sweet their mem'ry still!
> But they have left an aching void
> The world can never fill.
>
> Return, O Holy Dove, return,
> Sweet messenger of rest;
> I hate the sins that made Thee mourn
> And drove Thee from my breast.

One of my closest friends is a pilot. Some time ago he flew me to a Bible conference in a private plane. I'm somewhat of a frustrated pilot, and after we took off and were settled on course, I asked if I could take the controls. I thought I was doing pretty well until he tapped me on the shoulder and pointed at the compass. Without realising it, I had drifted far off course. In the same way, if we're not careful, we will assume we're right on the beam spiritually, when in fact we are drifting off course.

The stones were a witness to others

It has been said that you can't meet God and not know it. That's true. And others will know it too. When Moses came away from the presence of God, his face glowed with the glory of that encounter – and the people saw it. Describing the mercy of God, the psalmist wrote: 'And He put a new song in my mouth, a song of praise to our God; many will see and fear, and will trust in the Lord' (Psalm 40:3). There's an unusual song – you see it instead of hearing it. Neither the psalmist nor Moses had to convince people they had met God. Moses didn't need a glow-in-the-dark bumper sticker that said, 'I'm living in the SONshine.' Badges, beads and bumper stickers are fine, but if it takes those things to show I'm a Christian, then I'm not much of one.

We have an obligation to those around us and to those who come after us. Three times in Joshua 4 the people were commanded to explain the meaning of the stones when their children asked about them.

That tells me that there ought to be something in our lives that makes people ask questions. Usually, in our witnessing efforts, the most difficult problem is how to get started, how to bring the subject up without offending. Some Christians wear curious-looking pins, hoping someone will ask them what they mean and open the door to witnessing. There's nothing wrong with that, but it ought to be our Christlike life and not a pin that causes folk to ask questions. The apostle Peter told his readers:

'Sanctify Christ as Lord in your hearts, always being ready to make a defense to every one who asks you to give an account for the hope that is in you' (1 Peter 3:15). If Jesus is Lord, be ready. Sooner or later someone is going to ask you about it.

While Peter was delivering his well-prepared sermon, the congregation interrupted him, crying, 'What must we do?' What preacher wouldn't like to have that kind of response! Do you know what made them do that? It wasn't only Peter's sermon. They had seen something earlier in the behaviour of the Christians that caused them to ask, 'What does this mean?' It was the transformed lives of the believers that attracted their attention so Peter could preach to them.

It was the same with the Philippian jailer. He had been so impressed with the way Paul and Silas reacted to their mistreatment and imprisonment that when God shook the foundations for them, he brought up the subject.

But here is the significant thing about the stones. They were the past reaching into the present; a present condition resulting from a past event. It's all right to talk about the past if there is some evidence of that past in the present. Every once in a while someone says to me, 'You should have seen this church fifteen years ago. God sent a great revival – it was really something!' When I hear that I feel like saying, 'Well, I'm glad you told me, otherwise I'd never have known it.' There's nothing wrong with talking about the past – it's good to remember and recite God's past blessings. But here's the point: there ought to be present evidence of those past blessings. That past work of God should have been the beginning of an experience that is still going on.

Before we leave this subject, notice that each tribe had

a stone. This says to me that every family ought to have
a memorial of God's blessings. As the head of each tribe
was responsible for getting the stone, the head of each
family should be able to bring a stone representing his
experience with the Lord as a witness to his family. There
ought to be in his life something that makes his children
ask about his experience with the Lord.

When the stones were properly placed, God said they
would be a witness to all the world 'that all the peoples
of the earth may know that the hand of the Lord is
mighty' (Joshua 4:24). And as we learn to follow through
with our experience and go on to maturity in Christ, we
will become a memorial to the mighty, saving hand of our
Lord.

9

Why We Fail to Grow

Billy Sunday used to say, 'If we Christians were as weak physically as we are spiritually, we would all need crutches.' The colourful baseball-player-turned-evangelist was saying that if you're not growing spiritually, you ought to be worried. Growth is the normal and natural result of life, and if there isn't growth, that life is in jeopardy. We're not surprised when we grow physically; we expect it. If, by chance, growth doesn't occur, we immediately know something is wrong and attempt to uncover the problem.

And yet we often look upon Christians who have grown and are growing as extraordinary specimens of Christianity. As a pastor I was always excitedly surprised to find members who were really spiritual. They became the major sites of interest I pointed out to visiting ministers, who never failed to share my excitement and coveted the same phenomenon for their own church. But if I had driven him around town pointing out this person who had grown a couple of centimetres in the last year, and that one who had gained three kilograms, he would have thought me crazy.

I believe as Christians we have no right to call

ourselves normal until spiritual growth becomes as natural as physical growth. The apostle John prayed that his friend Gaius would prosper and be in good health, 'just as your soul prospers' (3 John 2). Would you want someone to pray the same thing for you? Frankly, if our physical and financial prosperity were determined by our spiritual prosperity, we would probably be crippled and bankrupt.

If growth is the normal consequence of life, then where's the problem? Just as there are enemies to physical growth, there are also enemies to spiritual growth. Our spiritual development is never unopposed. We do not simply drift into maturity. To grow we must swim upstream against the stubborn currents that try to hold us back. In the last chapter we discussed the follow-through of the Christian life. We saw that every authentic experience is a lasting one with continuing results.

OK, you accept that and desire it, but it isn't happening. You know your experience was real, and there has been some progress, but it is pitifully small, almost microscopic. What's the problem? The answer is the subject of this chapter. In this respect, Joshua 17 contains an instructive story. The people have entered the land and, according to God's instructions, Joshua is dividing it among the people. In verse 14 we hear a complaint from some of the tribes: 'Then the sons of Joseph spoke to Joshua, saying, "Why have you given me only one lot and one portion for an inheritance, since I am a numerous people whom the Lord has thus far blessed?"' Note the significant phrase 'thus far'. They are saying that in the past God had been good to them; up to this point the Lord has blessed them. The phrase implies some doubt about God's blessing from here on. Sounds like some of us, doesn't it? 'The Lord used to bless me, but something's happened. For a while everything was going so well, but now. . . .'

Get out your Bible and read Joshua 17:12–18. This passage throws some light on why we fail to grow.

We fail to grow when we exercise partial conquest

There's a telling statement in verses 12 and 13: 'But the sons of Manasseh could not take possession of these cities, because the Canaanites persisted in living in that land. And it came about when the sons of Israel became strong, they put the Canaanites to forced labor, *but they did not drive them out completely*' (author's emphasis).

Now don't miss this point: although Israel had conquered the land, many of the Canaanites – the enemy, if you like – still lived there. In Joshua 16:10, we read, 'But they [Manasseh and Ephraim] did not drive out the Canaanites who lived in Gezer, so the Canaanites live in the midst of Ephraim to this day, and they became forced laborers.' And over in Judges chapter 1 we discover an important clue concerning their problem.

> But Manasseh did not take possession of Bethshean . . . so the Canaanites persisted in living in that land. And it came about when Israel became strong, that they put the Canaanites to forced labor, but they did not drive them out completely. Neither did Ephraim drive out the Canaanites. . . . Zebulun did not drive out the inhabitants. . . . Asher did not drive out the inhabitants. . . . Naphtali did not drive out the inhabitants . . . (Judges 1: 27–31, 33)

Before Israel entered the land, God specified in no uncertain terms that all the inhabitants of the land were to be driven out completely – not a single Canaanite was to be left. But again and again, with monotonous significance, we read that they did not drive them out. Now the land teemed with both natives and newcomers. No wonder they complained of crowded conditions!

Suppose you meet me on the street and ask how I am.

'Not so well,' I answer. 'We need a larger house. There are only four of us, but we're crowded.'

'I can help you,' you say. 'There's a twelve-room house for sale for a really good price. A family of seven has lived there but they're wanting to move.'

'Thanks, I'll look into it.' Off I go and buy the house and move my wife and two children into the twelve rooms.

A few days later you meet me again on the street and ask how I am.

'Not so well,' I answer. 'We need a larger house.'

'A larger house? But there are only four of you in that twelve-room mansion! How could you be crowded?'

'Well, the former owners – seven of them, you know – are still living there, and it's pretty crowded.'

It wouldn't require a genius to solve my problem. Move out the former owners! What right do I have to complain about crowded conditions when I am not using the room I have?

And that was exactly the case with the complaining tribes. They had plenty of room, but it was occupied by the enemy. You see, it's foolish to ask God to give you more blessings when you haven't lived out the blessings you already have. It's no use asking God for additional truth when you haven't obeyed what you already know. My friend Manley Beasley was speaking to a ministers' meeting when he suddenly stopped and closed his Bible with this exclamation: 'That's enough preaching. You know more now than you're living up to!' Painfully true.

Let me put it to you in the phrase Alan Redpath used to describe this incident. 'Are you living up to your capacity?' Look around. Have you allowed some Canaanites to remain in your life? God told you to drive out every one, but there were two or three you were especially fond of and so you've allowed them to hang around. Of course, you've given them strict orders to behave themselves, and for the most part they've done so. Let me tell you, there can be no continuing growth as long as you tolerate the presence of a single Canaanite.

It's interesting to note some of the reasons we keep Canaanites around:

1. A spirit of compromise

God said that *every* inhabitant had to go. We reason that surely one or two won't make any difference. That's the way it begins. We know a thing is wrong – but just a little bit. And after all, no one is perfect; we know of worse things in some other Christians and they seem to get along OK. But no matter how we say it, we are compromising the word of God, and that is plain, unadulterated disobedience.

2. A spirit of complacency

Did you notice that when the tribes allowed the Canaanites to stay, they put them to forced labour? That means they made slaves of them. Yes, they had been the enemy, but now they were slaves and under control.

Who says the Bible isn't up-to-date? I can't count the number of people I've heard reason the same way. 'Yeah, I know it's not altogether right, but I can handle it. It's a problem, but I've learned to control it.' Have you ever heard someone say about his drinking, 'Oh, I can take it or leave it'? What's so great about that? That's all anyone can do – take it or leave it. There is no third alternative. But I have observed that those who say that usually choose to 'take it'.

The truth is, the Israelites couldn't handle it. The Canaanites refused to be slaves. And if the Israelites couldn't do it, neither can we.

3. A spirit of cowardice

If it weren't so tragic, this would be funny. Look at chapter 17, verse 16. Joshua had told the people that if they wanted more room, they should go up to the forest and clear the land. Here's their reply: 'And the sons of Joseph said, "The hill country is not enough for us, and all the Canaanites who live in the valley have chariots of iron. . . . "' There's the real reason. First they said that the hill country wasn't big enough, but actually they were afraid of the armed Canaanites. But I thought the Canaanites had been put to forced labour. I thought they were slaves and under control. If so, then those are the strangest slaves I've ever heard of!

Years ago I heard this story. I don't know whether it's true, but it's good. It seems that during a heavy battle, a captain commanded his lieutenant to pull back to a certain position. The lieutenant replied, 'I can't, sir.'

'Why not?' the captain asked.

'I've taken a prisoner, sir.'

'Bring him with you.'

'He won't come, sir.'

'Well, leave him and come yourself!'

'He won't let me, sir.'

One of the main reasons we don't try to drive out the Canaanites (those pet sins and hidden habits) is that we're afraid we can't. We avoid a direct confrontation. It's much more comfortable living with the illusion that we can drive them out any time we please. You say you can stop that habit any time you want to. Why don't you, then? Is it possible that you're the real slave?

4. A spirit of covetousness

'They put the Canaanites to forced labor.' Why drive them *all* out? They make good workers – and cheap labour. It could be very advantageous to keep a few of them around.

How does this apply to us? Here's a businessman who realises that it is the Lord who gives him the power to gain wealth, that it is actually his business; so he decides to operate on Christian principles. But in case God doesn't come through, he keeps a Canaanite of worldly business tactics in the back room.

Or perhaps a teenager commits himself to Christ and wants him to occupy first place in every area of his life. But it may be that being a Christian won't bring him everything he wants in popularity and pleasure, and so on occasions he resorts to a Canaanite of doubtful behaviour.

Maybe a pastor has decided that the gimmicks and gadgets he has been using to attract people to his church aren't Christ-honouring. From now on his ministry will be conducted solely on the principles the Holy Spirit approves. But the immediate visible results he had hoped for don't come. He was afraid that might happen and had cleverly kept one or two of the old Canaanite gimmicks around. They will build up that attendance in no time at all.

I think that's enough said. Are you living up to your capacity?

We fail to grow when we expect preferential consideration

Manasseh was the firstborn of Joseph; the Ephraimites were relatives of Joshua, the head man. Surely they deserved special treatment. You couldn't expect someone as great as they were to live by the same rules as everyone else. It was the VIP treatment for them.

I'm amazed at how many believers actually feel this way. They know the laws governing growth and spirituality – faithful Bible study and prayer, up-to-date confession of sin, diligent obedience to the word of God, God's glory desired in all things. And yet they expect God's blessings without them. As far as they're concerned, they have been lifted above the disciplines of discipleship. I've counselled Christians who had lost the joy of their salvation and wanted to recover it but refused to submit themselves to those disciplines. They were searching for an 'experience' that would catapult them effortlessly back into a right relationship with God.

Our passage reveals two factors that contribute to this attitude.

1. Arrogance

The sons of Joseph boasted that they were a great people and had been singularly blessed by the Lord. This, they thought, should qualify them for preferential treatment.

Pride is an insidious termite that eats away the foundation of Christian growth. It can attack a denomination, a church or an individual with equal deadliness. A denomination may assume it's great because it's big; a church because it's wealthy; a person because he's talented. Blessings can easily become curses. A respected position in the church, widely acclaimed talent, past blessings, high honours – any one of these can inflate us with the hot air of arrogance.

2. Indolence

This was touched upon in Chapter 2 but bears repeating. I'm convinced the main reason Christians are not more spiritual, more mature, more dedicated, is that they are too lazy! That's right. The major problem with most Christians is laziness. It was so with the crowd in Joshua 17. Joshua told them that if they wanted more land, they could have it if they were willing to work for it. Cut down the trees and drive out the Canaanites were the only stipulations. But that's exactly what they weren't willing to do. They didn't want to build or battle; they just wanted to beg. And we're often the same way. At this precise moment we are as spiritual as we really want to be. Oh, I know we moan and groan, wishing we were more spiritual; but wishing won't get it. It's useless to beg God for more growth if we're not willing to build and battle for it.

One day a father took his son to Spurgeon's College to study for the ministry under that prince of preachers. When Mr Spurgeon told the father the course of instruction would require several years, the father said, 'My son is an unusually bright young man. I'm certain you could arrange for him to finish much sooner.'

Mr Spurgeon replied, 'Sir, God takes twenty years to grow an oak tree and only six months to grow a squash. Which do you want your son to be?'

There are no short-cuts to maturity. To reach it demands discipline and determination. And that's what we are going to discuss now.

We fail to grow when we evade priority commitments

Here was Joshua's solution to their problem:

> And Joshua spoke to the house of Joseph, to Ephraim and Manasseh, saying, 'You are a numerous people and have great power; you shall not have one lot only, but the hill country shall be yours. For though it is a forest, you shall clear it, and to its farthest borders it shall be yours; for you shall drive out the Canaanites, even though they have chariots of iron and though they are strong.' (Joshua 17: 17–18)

Clear out the forest and drive out the Canaanites. That was the simple solution to their growth problem. But as we've already seen in the first chapter of Judges, they refused to accept his answer. Priority number one, according to Joshua, was to accomplish these two things. Until then, no expansion could be expected. The land was theirs, but before they could possess it, these things had to be done. So it is with us.

Although they evaded this priority commitment, I trust we will not. So let's examine more closely the two tasks Joshua assigned to them. I call them *priority commitments for growth*, as necessary to our growth as they were to theirs.

1. We must clear out the harmless things that clutter our lives

The first step was the clearing of the forest. Now there's nothing wrong with trees; they are a beautiful and useful part of God's creation. But if they occupy the ground you want to build your home on, they have to go. Building your home is a priority commitment, and in order to fulfil it, you must clear the land.

The trees symbolise the many harmless things, even good things, that fill the agenda of our daily lives. I'm certain that when we've talked about the necessity of a daily time of prayer and Bible study, someone has said, 'Oh, that would be great, but I'm just too busy. I don't have room for another thing in my day.' The truth is, we all have the same amount of time: twenty-four hours to the day and seven days to the week. I find that people usually manage to make time for what they think is really important. And if you don't have time to do everything God intends you to do, it simply means that you are misusing some of your time. There is time to do everything you are supposed to do. The trouble is that most of us are so busy being good, we don't have time to be godly.

In Matthew 13, Jesus described this situation in the parable of the sower. It is really a parable of the soil, for the soil is the main subject of the story. The part that concerns us tells about the seed that fell into thorny ground: 'And others fell among the thorns, and the thorns came up and choked them out' (Matthew 13:7). Jesus explains the meaning in verse 22: 'And the one on whom seed was sown among the thorns, this is the man who hears the word, and the worry of the world, and the deceitfulness of riches choke the word, and it becomes unfruitful.' The ground of his life was so cluttered with the cares of this world, the word of God was strangled before it had a chance to grow. What a description of so many! No wonder the word of God never produces anything fruitful and lasting in their lives – it can't compete with the thorns.

You will never *find* time for God; you will have to *make* time. This means some trees will have to be cut down. Perhaps late-night television will have to be eliminated so you can rise earlier in order to have time to pray and read the word. That's only an example of what I mean. If you really want to know, God will show you the trees you need to clear away.

2. We must clean out the harmful things that corrupt our lives

After the trees come the Canaanites. Let me point out something interesting. It would seem more reasonable to drive out the Canaanites first. After all, do you think they're going to lounge around watching us chop down those trees? No. All the Canaanites in the world will come swooping down upon us. But Joshua did have them in the correct order. Cut down the trees, then you will be able to drive out the enemy.

You will never have the power to drive out the habits and leftover sins in your life until you give priority to a daily time of fellowship and communion with God. Once you have accomplished this, the divine strength you receive will enable you to drive out the enemy. Remember, in Chapter 7 we saw that although Israel entered the land ready to fight, the first thing God had the nation do was worship. That's the divine order: worship before warfare.

The principle of growth lives within every believer, but as with our physical development, we must co-operate with the laws of spiritual health if that growth is to be realised.

10

Will It Last?

When I first encountered this 'victorious life', my immediate question was, 'Will it last?' I didn't actually ask anyone the question because I was afraid I already knew the answer. Since becoming a Christian I had had plenty of mountain-top experiences, each time thinking, 'This is it! At last I've got it!' (whatever *it* was). But like a hot fuse on a dud firecracker, the experiences started with a sizzle and ended with a fizzle. Welcome back to the valley of despair. And each malfunction left that valley a little deeper, a little darker and a lot drier.

I was weary of lugging buckets of water from the wells of others. Jesus had promised me my own well of living water. But I didn't know where to dig.

Will it last? Perhaps the same question keeps badgering you. You may even feel like the college student who told me, 'I've had it with you preachers! Each one that comes to town has a different formula for living the Christian life. And I've tried 'em all. And you know what? They don't work. It never lasts. A couple of weeks and I'm right back where I started. I'm tired of trying and failing, trying and failing.'

He wasn't being rude, just honest. And I knew exactly

how he felt. But it doesn't have to be that way. The real
thing will last ... *if* we understand that there is no such
thing in the Christian life as a 'quick fix'; that there is no
instant cure-all that solves all things for always; that there
is no once-for-all experience that produces a short-cut on
the road to maturity.

One question, two answers

So the big question is, 'Will it last?' And the answer is
yes – and no. Don't let the 'no' scare you off; it's not as
bad as it may seem. Actually, the 'no' is necessary if there
is to be a 'yes'. Part of the experience does not last and
part of it does. And the part that does not makes possible
the part that does.

The part that does not last is our present level of
commitment. The part that does last is the progressing
level of commitment.

First, let's look at the present level of commitment.
When the Holy Spirit confronted me with the lordship of
Christ and his promise of daily victory, I responded with
a total commitment of myself to him. As far as I was
aware, God had all of me there was to have. It was, in
truth, a total commitment – and yet it was incomplete.

Two things are essential to commitment: knowledge of
ourselves and knowledge of the Lord. In commitment we
yield all that we know of ourselves to all that we know of
him. And while that commitment may be total, it is
incomplete. Why? Because commitment is limited by
knowledge – knowledge of ourselves and knowledge of
him. And since that knowledge is incomplete, our
commitment likewise is incomplete. That is why our
present level of commitment cannot, must not, remain the

same. 'We may choose death once for all in some solemn hour of consecration, but we only gradually come to learn all that involves.'[1]

Through time and experience we discover new things about ourselves and the Lord. As this happens, we must bring these things under his lordship. For example, we will learn some things about ourselves — a painfully disturbing experience. When we are basking in the warm sun of victory, we're certain that every sin, every fault, every unholy habit has been crushed beneath the heel of our Deliverer. Then suddenly a weed of the old life reappears. There it is, sprouting up through the earth as though carefully and painstakingly cultivated. It may be an unexpected and unChristian attitude, a resentment long forgotten, a habit once overcome.

What has happened? Does this mean our experience was false, our victory an illusion? No, not at all. This is simply one of the ways God moves us from our present level of commitment. He knows what monsters lurk beneath the surface of our heart and he exposes them so we may deal with them. Again, F. B. Meyer writes, 'It is only as the clearer light of heaven falls upon us that we come to see the true nature of many things which we had counted innocent, and hugged as dearer than life.'[2]

Also we discover that the boundaries of Christ's lordship take in more territory than we first imagined, and each such discovery requires an update in our commitment to him. Keeping our commitment up to date is an essential part of making the victorious life a lasting experience. Paul gives us a beautiful picture of how this works in Romans 6:17: 'But thanks be to God that though you were slaves of sin, you became obedient from the heart to that form of teaching to which you were committed.' The phrase, 'to which you were committed', means literally 'to which you were handed over, to which you were delivered'. And the word translated 'form' is 'mould' or 'pattern'. It is the kind of form or mould you pour cement or plaster of Paris into. Paul says we have been delivered or handed over to a certain form or mould of teaching.

A few years ago my father put in a tennis court on the family 'farm' in Arkansas and I watched the workmen build it. After the ground was properly prepared, they used some old wooden planks to build a form. The form was the exact size and shape of a tennis court. But it wasn't a tennis court, just a load of planks forming a perfect outline of a court. When the form was finished and in place, a cement mixer truck came out to the place, backed up to the form, and delivered the cement to the form of truth. And do you know what the cement did? It obeyed the form. It allowed the form to direct its flow and design its shape. The movement of the cement was confined to the boundaries of the form, and when it was hardened it looked exactly as the form intended.

In the same way God has a form of truth for us – the word of God. And he is constantly delivering us to the form, handing us over to the shaping influence of the word; and like that cement, we are to obey the form, allowing it to direct and design our lives. And when it is finished, we will look as the form intended.

You see, God doesn't reveal the whole truth to us at once. We couldn't take it. But he gives it to us in doses we can handle. At first he feeds us with milk, then later with meat. That's why the present level of commitment, regardless of how complete we think it is, cannot last.

New generation, old gods

There is an illuminating statement in Joshua 24:14. Joshua, now an old man, is delivering his farewell address to his people. Suddenly he confronts them with this challenge: 'Now, therefore . . . put away the gods which your fathers served beyond the River and in Egypt.' *Put away the gods of Egypt!* Remember that the entire generation that came out of Egypt, with the exception of Joshua and Caleb, had died in the wilderness. The present generation, the one Joshua is addressing, had been born and reared in the wilderness. They had never set foot in Egypt. And yet these people, who had never been to Egypt, had traces of Egypt in their lives. A whole generation separated them from Egypt, but Egypt was still very much with them. One would think that after forty years the Egyptian weeds would have died out. But Joshua knew that in spite of the passing years there still existed among his people a strong tendency towards idolatry. He sensed the suppressed fire within them that could at any moment burst into a blaze.

No matter how long you have been a Christian, no matter how long you have lived in the land of victory, you must still grapple with the weeds of the old life. The gods of Egypt, sometimes silently but always cleverly, will try to take fresh root in your life. When that happens, you will be faced with a decision. Will you decisively and harshly deal with them, hurling them under the conquering foot of the Lord? If you do, you will rise to a new level of commitment. But if you succumb to the old gods, if you allow the weeds to flourish, you will find yourself back in the wilderness of defeat, moaning to yourself, 'It didn't last.'

Now let's look at the flip side, the progressive level of commitment. Once we realise that we cannot remain at our present level of commitment, God will be able to take us on to higher plateaux of surrender. Throughout our Christian life we will encounter testing and temptations designed to challenge our earlier decision. Did I really mean it when I said, 'Everything, Lord'? Our adversary, the devil, is a bad loser, and, following every victory you experience in Christ, he will mount a counterattack to recapture lost ground. This will force you to reaffirm your commitment to Christ. Such confrontations enlarge your capacity for God, giving him more working room in your life. So it is good to view these times of testing as a call from God to a new level of commitment.

The key, therefore, to ensuring a continuing life of victory is to keep your commitment up to date.

And how we keep it up to date Joshua tells us in this twenty-fourth chapter. The wily warrior, ever alert to the dangers that surrounded his people, challenges them to rise to a new level of commitment. Only this, he claims, will assure their continued possession of the land. They must not take Canaan for granted. And neither must we take for granted our victory in Christ. We, like Israel, can be evicted from that fair and flowering land.

Verse 14 is the heart of Joshua's message. It contains three commands – commands which, when obeyed, make possible a lasting experience of victory in Christ: 'Now, therefore, fear the Lord and serve Him, in sincerity and truth; and put away the gods which your fathers served beyond the River and in Egypt, and serve the Lord.'

'Fear the Lord'

This is the basic attitude God desires in every heart. 'Fearing the Lord' sums up the religious disposition God expected of the Old Testament believer. Fear is to the Old Testament what faith is to the New. If Joshua had been using New Testament terminology, he would have said, 'Have faith in God.' Like faith, the fear of the Lord should possess and pervade the life of every believer.

Sometime when you have a dozen hours to spare, get a concordance and look up all the references in the Bible to 'fearing the Lord'. I think you will be amazed, as I was, at the tremendous emphasis God places on the subject. Here are just a few references:

- 'The secret of the Lord is for those who fear Him, and He will make them know His covenant' (Psalm 25:14).
- 'How great is Thy goodness, which Thou hast stored up for those who fear Thee' (Psalm 31:19).
- 'Behold, the eye of the Lord is on those who fear Him' (Psalm 33:18).
- 'He will bless those who fear the Lord' (Psalm 115:13).
- 'The Lord favors those who fear Him' (Psalm 147:11).

But a part of us instinctively rebels against the idea of 'fearing God'. Ours is a religion of love, not fear. How can we be afraid of someone who loves us and whom we love? This assumed contradiction is resolved when we remember that there are different kinds of fear.

First, there is *superstitious* fear, which is the fruit of

ignorance. This is the fear that touches wood and avoids walking under ladders and opening umbrellas inside the house. Such fear is alien to the Christian faith.

Unfortunately, many people, even Christians, are infected with this kind of fear. In one of my conferences a minister wanted to buy some Bible study cassettes that cost thirteen dollars. 'Can I make out the cheque for twelve dollars,' he asked, 'and owe you a dollar?' It was such an unusual request, I asked why. He said he felt it bad luck to write a cheque for thirteen dollars. I couldn't believe it. This was a minister of the gospel, and the tapes he wanted were studies on the devil, demons and the occult. I almost gave him the tapes – he really needed them. Instead I said, 'Tell you what. Make out the cheque for fourteen and I'll owe *you* a dollar.' And he did.

There are sad chapters in church history in which large segments of Christianity were nothing more than strongholds of superstition. They propagated the gospel of superstition instead of the gospel of salvation. Unfortunately some believers still tend to confuse superstitious fear with godly fear. While waiting at Charles DeGaulle Airport in Paris for a flight to Geneva along with a group of Christians, one of our party suddenly realised that our flight number was 666. We had a near mutiny on our hands when several insisted we wait for the next flight.

One Christian worker told me, in all seriousness, that he believed a series of meetings he had participated in had failed because the pastor of the church drove a Plymouth Demon.

This fear is definitely not 'the beginning of wisdom' (Proverbs 9:10).

Then there is *slavish* or *servile* fear, an inordinate fear of punishment. This fear causes us to cower before God as though he were a cruel and capricious tyrant. But we are not to fear the Lord like the slave of a sadistic master who trembles whenever summoned into his presence. Slavish fear never produces faithful and loving servants.

Finally, there is *scriptural* or *filial* fear, which has its springs in love. It is the attitude of awe and reverence befitting a child for its parent. This is a healthy, wholesome fear that is careful not to offend, and is diligent to please. For example, God has blessed me with a wife and children whom I love with all my heart. To me they are my most precious possessions in life. The thought of betraying their trust or forfeiting their respect by unworthy behaviour is unbearable. That is *filial* fear.

This is the fear with which we are to 'fear the Lord', and it involves three things. First, it means to remember the Lord, remembering when we sit down to our dinner tables that it is the Lord who has provided the food; remembering when we receive our pay cheque that it is the Lord who gives us the health and energy to work; remembering when we lie down to sleep that our lives are in his gracious hands. Either we fear him or we forget him.

To fear the Lord is to reverence him, to hold his holiness in high esteem and to reflect that holiness in all our actions. It is this fear, this reverential awe, that causes men to worship and adore him.

A classic example of reverential fear is found in the response of the disciples when Jesus exercised his authority over the storm-tossed sea in the fourth chapter of Mark. As the disciples crossed the sea a violent storm suddenly engulfed their ship. The disciples were swamped with terror, while Jesus was sound asleep.

Shaking him awake, they cried, 'Master, carest thou not that we perish?' Jesus immediately rebuked the storm, and then rebuked the disciples: 'Why are ye so fearful? How is it that ye have no faith?' Jesus rebuked their fear, which was a cowardly, intimidating fear. But the next verse says, 'And they feared exceedingly, and said one to another, What manner of man is this, that even the wind and the sea obey him?' (Mark 4:37–41, KJV).

Notice the two fears of the disciples: one was caused by the storm and condemned by Jesus. But there was a second fear caused by the stilling of the storm, a majestic display of Christ's power. They literally 'feared with a great fear'. But no condemnation falls upon this fear, for this is the fear of reverential awe. Christ's authority over the wind and the waves filled them with a new reverence and respect for their Master.

When Gypsy Smith was asked the secret of his long and vibrant Christian life, the old veteran evangelist said, 'I never lost the wonder.'

And finally, to fear the Lord is to recognise his authority in our lives. To fear God is to obey him. This was the response the congregation made to Joshua's appeal: 'We will serve the Lord our God and we will obey His voice' (Joshua 24:24). As far back as Deuteronomy 6:2, Moses made it clear that fear of God and obedience were inseparably linked together: 'So that you and your son and your grandson might fear the Lord your God, to keep all His statutes and His commandments, which I command you, all the days of your life, and that your days may be prolonged.'

To fear God is to acknowledge that he has the right to command us; a right founded on the fact that he has created us, he has redeemed us and he sustains us. These facts formed the basis of Joshua's challenge to the people. The first thirteen verses of chapter 24 are a magnificent account of the wonderful things God had done for his people. Who could refuse to fear God after that? Who else could equal his claim to their obedient devotion?

'Serve the Lord'

This command and the one following – 'Put away' – are the practical expressions of the fear of the Lord. Godly fear manifests itself in service to God and in separation from other gods.

Serving the Lord is the positive issue of fearing the Lord. But it is more than simply working for the Lord. The Hebrew word means 'to pay homage' and contains the ideas of both work and worship. It implies a claim accepted and an allegiance pledged. When one serves the Lord it means he has acknowledged the Lord's claim to his life, love and loyalty, and serves him to the exclusion of all others.

Exclusively his – this is what Joshua meant when he called the people to serve the Lord. The issue was not just service, but service to whom? For serve they would. All men are servants of some god. The only question is, which god?

> Choose for yourselves today whom you will serve: whether the gods which your fathers served which were beyond the River, or the gods of the Amorites in whose land you are living; but as for me and my house, we will serve the Lord. (Joshua 24:15)

'Choose for yourselves today whom you will serve.' The root idea of the Hebrew word 'choose' is 'to take a keen look at', and implies a testing or examining. It is a penetrating, distinguishing examination that lies at the heart of the choosing. This choice is not made lightly, flippantly or blindly. God isn't afraid to be compared with other gods. In Exodus 8:10 Moses makes it clear that God intends to prove there is no other god like him. Moses promises to remove the plague of frogs from Pharaoh's people so that 'you may know that there is no one like the Lord our God'.

After the deliverance at the Red Sea, Moses and the sons of Israel sang, 'Who is like Thee among the gods, O Lord? Who is like Thee, majestic in holiness, awesome in praises, working wonders?' (Exodus 15:11).

The psalmist declared, 'There is no one like Thee among the gods, O Lord; nor are there any works like Thine' (Psalm 86:8).

But it is through the prophet Isaiah that the real challenges to compare gods are hurled at the people. After an exquisite portrayal of the Lord God and his works, the prophet cries, 'To whom will you liken God? Or what likeness will you compare with Him?' (Isaiah 40:18).

' "To whom then will you liken Me that I should be his equal?" says the Holy One' (Isaiah 40:25).

Isaiah 46 is a classic satirical comparison between the false gods of Babylon and the true God of Israel. First, Isaiah describes the efforts of Babylonians to save their gods when Cyrus overruns the country. 'Bel has bowed down, Nebo stoops over; their images are consigned to the beasts and the cattle. The things that you carry are burdensome, a load for the weary beast. . . . They lift it [their god] upon the shoulder and carry it; they set it in its place and it stands there. It does not move from its place'

(Isaiah 46:1, 7). A false god must be carried by its worshippers and is limited by their own strength.

But not so the true God, the God of Israel: 'Listen to Me, O house of Jacob, and all the remnant of the house of Israel, you who have been borne by me from birth, and have been carried from the womb; even to your old age, I shall be the same, and even to your graying years I shall bear you . . . and I shall deliver you' (Isaiah 46:3–4). The true God, rather than being carried, carries his people and is in no way fettered by their weakness or weariness.

> To whom would you liken Me,
> And make Me equal and compare Me
> That we should be alike? (Isaiah 46:5)

'Bring me your best gods,' dares the Lord, 'and I will beat them all.' He knows that if the people compare him with other gods, only one reasonable choice can be made.

Just as there were other claimants for the service of Israel back then – the Chaldean and Egyptian and Amorite gods – there is a multitude of gods today vying for our service. And a dozen times a day we must choose whom we will serve – the gods of the flesh, of lust, of greed, of revenge, of ambition, or the God of our Lord Jesus Christ. Again, the issue is not *will* we serve, but *whom* will we serve?

This service is to be with sincerity. This interesting Hebrew word was used of animals which were without blemish. It meant to be complete, whole or entire, with nothing lacking. The word referred to the harmony between external and internal qualities. In other words, our outward service is to be a true reflection of the inward dedication.

Isaiah's words illustrate the point: 'Then the Lord said, "Because this people draw near with their words and honor Me with their lip service, but they remove their hearts far from Me"' (Isaiah 29:13).

'And truth,' Joshua adds. This was the word Rahab the harlot used when she asked for a pledge of truth from the spies (Joshua 2:12), a sign that could be counted on. Firmness, faithfulness and certainty are the ideas contained in the word. To serve the Lord in truth means to serve him with a fierce loyalty that can always be counted upon.

Our service must be personal, an individual choice. Joshua said, 'But as for me and my house, we will serve the Lord' (Joshua 24:15). Whatever others may do, whatever gods others may serve, I will serve the Lord, says Joshua. And we must always be prepared to stand alone in our commitment to Christ. I'm reminded of Peter's question to Jesus in John 21:21. Jesus has graciously reinstated the fallen apostle to his former position of leadership and now commands him, 'Follow Me.' Suddenly Peter sees John walking behind them, and asks, 'Lord, and what about this man?' Jesus kept the focus on Peter by saying, 'If I want him to remain until I come, what is that to you? You follow Me!' (John 21:22). Like Peter we hesitate, wondering what our friends will do, which gods they will choose. 'What is that to you? You follow Me!'

Whose life is it anyway?

The New Testament counterpart to Joshua's challenge is Paul's words to the Corinthians: 'Or do you not know that your body is a temple of the Holy Spirit who is in you, whom you have from God, and that you are not your own? For you have been bought with a price: therefore glorify God in your body' (1 Corinthians 6:19–20).

These two verses occupy a strategic position in the life of victory. The Corinthians were a carnal bunch. Although Paul addresses them as 'saints' in his opening greeting (1 Corinthians 1:2), he later describes them as 'fleshly'; believers behaving like unbelievers (1 Corinthians 3:1–4). To Paul falls the Herculean task of bringing them from carnality to spirituality. And his strategy is to fiercely remind them that they have been bought and paid for by the blood of Christ; and so, belonging to him, they owe him exclusive allegiance.

I'm convinced that many people believe the Bible because they don't know what it says. For instance, did you know that the Bible says, 'You are not your own'? That's not just religious talk – that's literal truth. We have been purchased by the blood of Christ. He owns us, lock, stock and barrel. We don't have a right to our own life because it is no longer ours. It is his. As a matter of fact, the believer has no personal rights. He is the bond slave of Jesus Christ, and his only right is to please his Master.

The Corinthians thought they had the right to live as they pleased. They failed to realise that they no longer belonged to themselves. And that is a carnal Christian: one who believes he has a right to his own life.

This being so, Paul reasons, our bodies are to be used exclusively for his glory. Our lives are the instruments of his will, the display case in which he manifests his glory.

Note the logical sequence of Paul's words: (1) You are not your own; (2) you are the temple of the Holy Spirit; (3) therefore, glorify God in your body. I usually shy away from neat little formulas, but I have translated

Paul's words into a triplet that helps me keep in focus my relationship to God. Perhaps you'll find it helpful.

> I must admit his possession of my body.
> I must acknowledge his presence in my body.
> I must accept his purpose for my body.

'Put away'

This was the third part of Joshua's challenge to the people: 'Put away the gods which your fathers served beyond the River and in Egypt.' Here is the negative issue of fearing the Lord.

The people made a speedy response to Joshua's words. 'And the people answered and said, "Far be it from us that we should forsake the Lord to serve other gods. . . . We also will serve the Lord, for He is our God"' (Joshua 24:16, 18).

Actually their response was a little too speedy for Joshua's liking, for in verse 19 we read, 'Then Joshua said to the people, "You will not be able to serve the Lord, for He is a holy God. He is a jealous God; He will not forgive your transgression or your sins."'

This old seasoned veteran recognised a hasty and careless decision when he saw one. His stern and repelling word were meant to rebuke their offhanded and easy commitment and to point out how serious such vows were. For God takes our vows seriously, whether we do or not.

But the people insist that they will serve the Lord. So, in effect, Joshua says, 'Prove it. Prove you are serious about your commitment. Do something practical to demonstrate your vow. Put away the foreign gods which are in your midst. Clean out your houses and your hearts. Throw out everything that is alien to your allegiance to the Lord God.'

Lightly made vows have haunted Christianity from its beginning. Jesus refused glib vows and still does so today. He wants no soldiers enlisting under false pretences or with thoughtless assumptions.

How to put away false gods

As we stated earlier, old gods are like weeds that reappear year after year. They have more lives than a cat and cling to us like goose grass to a sweater. How do we overcome when we are overwhelmed?

Good old Joshua – how well he understood the human heart. To his command to put away the foreign gods, he adds another, which is more than just another command. It reveals the way in which the former command can be obeyed effectively: 'Now therefore, put away the foreign gods which are in your midst, and *incline your hearts to the Lord*, the God of Israel' (Joshua 24:23, emphasis added).

'Incline your hearts to the Lord.' Most scholars agree that the gods to which Joshua refers are not actual idols of wood or stone or metal. These material representations have probably long since been destroyed. But the gods they symbolised still have a hold on their hearts. These are not idols of stone but idols of the heart – or as Calvin called them 'figments of false gods'.

Joshua knew that the heart of the problem was the problem of the heart. Even in the negative action of putting away their hidden gods, there must be a positive activity of inclining their hearts towards the Lord. The Hebrew word 'incline' is a picturesque one, meaning 'to

extend, to stretch out, to bend'. It is the word of the
psalmist when he prays, 'Incline my heart to Thy
testimonies' (Psalm 119:36), the idea being 'let me bend
all my thoughts in that one direction'.[3] The expression 'to
incline the ear' is found several times in Jeremiah (7:24,
26; 11:8, 17:23) and means to listen obediently to the
voice of God.

What Joshua is saying is that it does no good to drive
the evil spirits out of the house if the house is left vacant.
Something must fill the void created by putting away the
false gods. And only as the heart is bent, stretched, in the
direction of the Lord, with his word and his will
occupying the premises, will the life be safe from the
enemy's counterattack.

Will it last? I have made the joyful discovery that the real
thing does last. And it doesn't merely last, it grows bigger
and better. I no longer lug buckets of water from the wells
of others. Jesus has given me an Artesian well that
requires neither rope nor bucket. The living waters spring
up to meet me. It is a well that never runs dry, even in the
darkest moments of life. In the years since that
experience of entering in, I have trudged through a desert
where no water was, where no flowers grew, where
cherished voices no longer greeted me – but the well was
there. I am happy to report that through disappointment,
frustration, heartbreak, tragedy and death, the experience
has lasted. And today my knowledge of, fellowship with
and joy in Jesus are sweeter than ever before. I expect it
to be more so tomorrow.

I heard about two hippies on an ocean voyage.
Standing at the rail of the ship staring at the vast expanse
of endless sea, one said, 'Man, dig all that crazy water.'

The other, mesmerised by the view, said, 'Yeah, and that's only the top!' And in the Christian life, this life of victory, we have touched only the top. There is more to Jesus than any of us has ever experienced, and throughout eternity we will drink deeper and deeper from the inexhaustible fountain of his matchless grace.

The book is ended but the journey is not. I think it may end like this:

> Who is this who comes to meet me
>   On the desert way,
> As the Morning Star foretelling
>   God's unclouded day?
> He it is who came to win me
>   On the cross of shame;
> In His glory well I know Him
>   Evermore the same.
>
> Oh, the blessed joy of meeting,
>   All the desert past!
> Oh, the wondrous words of greeting
>   He shall speak at last!
> He and I together entering
>   Those fair courts above —
> He and I together sharing
>   All the Father's love.
>
> Where no shade nor stain can enter,
>   Nor the gold be dim,
> In that holiness unsullied,
>   I shall walk with Him.
> Meet companion then for Jesus,
>   From Him, for Him, made —
> Glory of God's grace forever
>   There in me displayed.

He who in His hour of sorrow
  Bore the curse alone;
I who through the lonely desert
  Trod where He had gone;
He and I, in that bright glory,
  One deep joy shall share —
Mine, to be forever with Him;
  His, that I am there.
                    Gerhard Tersteegen

Notes

1. F. B. Meyer, *Joshua* (Christian Literature Crusade, 1977),
   p. 204.
2. *Ibid*.
3. H. C. Leupold, *Exposition of Psalms* (The Wartburg Press,
   1959), p. 831.

Will God Heal Me?

by Ronald Dunn

As a pastor, Ronald Dunn has prayed for the sick and seen them healed; and he has prayed and seen them die. There have been times when he has known a special assurance that healing would come, and others when events have been almost impossible to understand.

Explanations abound, for we all want to know why God doesn't always heal. We are told to have more faith, to confess our sins, or to claim our inheritance. But such explanations usually add to the burdens of both the sick and those who care for them. They are *partly* correct, but there is no greater danger to truth than *partial* truth.

This book will take the pressure off those who do not feel they are allowed to be ill. It is replete with true stories, but these are examined in the light of the Bible's teaching, lest we be eager to turn experience into doctrine.

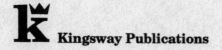 **Kingsway Publications**